TUTOR

A COLLABORATIVE APPROACH TO LITERACY INSTRUCTION

By

Judy Blankenship Cheatham, Ph.D.
Greensboro College, Greensboro, NC

Ruth Johnson Colvin, Founder
Literacy Volunteers of America, Inc.

Lester L. Laminack, Ed.D.
Western Carolina University, Cullowhee, NC

New Readers Press
Division of ProLiteracy Worldwide

All proceeds from the sale of this book go to further the work of ProLiteracy Worldwide. This seventh edition of **TUTOR** includes material from the previous editions by Ruth Colvin and Jane Root, Ph.D.

New Readers Press
Division of ProLiteracy Worldwide
1320 Jamesville Avenue, Syracuse, New York 13210

20 19 18 17 16 15 14

ISBN 1-56853-362-4
Order #91088

PROJECT COORDINATOR AND PRODUCTION EDITOR: SHARON HACHEY
DRAFT EDITORS: ROBERTA R. ARMSTRONG, Ph.D.; GEORGE D. CHEATHAM, Ph.D.; V.K. LAWSON, Ph.D.
DESIGN AND ORGANIZATION: PIKE DESIGN + COPY, FAYETTEVILLE, NEW YORK

ABOUT THE AUTHORS

JUDY BLANKENSHIP CHEATHAM, Ph.D., Writing Consultant

Judy Cheatham has worked with family and workplace literacy since 1986 in projects underwritten by grants from the National Endowment for the Humanities, the U. S. Department of Education, the Kentucky Humanities Council, and the Kentucky Literacy Commission. She has implemented two workplace programs and serves as a consultant to several others. Presently, she directs an Even Start Family Literacy Program and serves on several literacy boards. Dr. Cheatham holds a Ph.D. in Writing Theory and Instruction from the University of Mississippi. An Associate Professor of English, she is the Campbell Professor of Writing at Greensboro College, North Carolina. She is co-author of *Small Group Tutoring: A Collaborative Approach for Literacy Instruction* as well as several articles on American literature.

RUTH JOHNSON COLVIN, Founder

Ruth Colvin is the Founder and served as the first President of Literacy Volunteers of America, Inc. (LVA). At present she is Chair of the Research and Development Committee and the International Committee. She continues to be active as a volunteer tutor in both Basic Literacy and English as a Second Language (ESL), reaching out to adapt new methods to LVA's one-to-one and small group tutoring. Ruth Colvin and Jane Root, Ph.D., were the authors of the original *TUTOR* and its six revisions.

Since 1962, when Mrs. Colvin started LVA, she and her husband, Bob, have traveled all over the United States and the world giving Basic Literacy and English as a Second Language tutor training workshops. The recipient of seven honorary Doctor of Humane Letters degrees, Mrs. Colvin was awarded the United States of America's President's Volunteer Action Award in 1987, the nation's highest award given to a volunteer. She was inducted into the National Women's Hall of Fame in 1993.

Mrs. Colvin is also author or co-author of:

I Speak English, a handbook for teachers of conversational English

READ, an assessment tool for adult new readers

A Way With Words, the story of Literacy Volunteers of America

Great Traveling After 55, a "how to" book for veteran as well as new travelers

LESTER L. LAMINACK, Ed.D., Reading Consultant

Lester Laminack is a professor at Western Carolina University in North Carolina. He teaches graduate and undergraduate courses in Early Childhood Education and Reading. He has published numerous articles in *The Reading Teacher, Language Arts, Young Children* and *Science and Children*. He has also written *Reading With Children*, a book with accompanying video which offers ideas and reading activities to tutors for using children's literature to enhance the reading skills of children and their parents. Dr. Laminack has recently been chosen as chair of the Department of Elementary Education and Reading at Western Carolina University, North Carolina.

ACKNOWLEDGMENTS

In 1972, Jane Root, Ph.D., and Ruth Colvin, LVA Founder, collaborated on the first edition of *TUTOR*. Over the next 15 years, Jane and Ruth reissued five more editions. We gratefully acknowledge what has gone before as we introduce *TUTOR 7*.

We would like to thank those people and institutions that have helped make this 7th Edition of *TUTOR* much better than it would have been otherwise. In the Syracuse area, Ruth is especially indebted to the individual students and small groups with whom she has worked for over 30 years; these have provided her an opportunity to work through much of what is discussed in the following pages as well as the insights to write, with Jane Root, the first six editions of *TUTOR*.

In Greensboro, Judy thanks the over 200 tutors she has trained through Reading Connections, Inc.; these last two years of trainings have provided her with first-hand knowledge of tutors' responses and requests as well as allowed her the opportunity for her own field testing. Through the generous endowment of Ruth and Jack Campbell, Greensboro College has allowed Judy the time to devote her talents to these humanitarian pursuits.

In Cullowhee, Lester thanks the host of elementary education majors and reading teachers with whom he has formulated, discussed, and refined his own theories of language and learning. Western Carolina University has graciously shared Lester and his talents with the Literacy Volunteers community.

On a national level, we thank the staff, especially Sharon Hachey, who has spent many a 24-hour day working on this publication, and the Volunteers in Technical Assistance (V.I.T.A.) Corps, who have tirelessly read and re-read our many drafts, especially Phyllis Anderson, Dorothy Clark, and Chloe Fessler.

Finally, we are indeed indebted to all the students, tutors, trainers, and program coordinators from across the country who have helped us in preparing this latest edition of *TUTOR*. We appreciate the diligence of Marj Johnson and the rest of the support staff. We extend a special thanks to these literacy professionals for their review: Katy Cave, Lexington, KY; Valerie Meyer, Ph.D., Southern Illinois University at Edwardsville; Judie Thelen, Ph.D., Frostburg University of Maryland; Terilyn Turner, Ph.D., Lifelong Literacy; and Susan Vogel, Ph.D., Northern Illinois University. Whatever flaws remain, of course, are ours alone.

Over the past 30 months, we have spent many hours away from our families while we wrote as a team. Although difficult at times, Zachary and Glenda Laminack; George, Dayton, and Sarah Hampton Cheatham; and Bob Colvin have always supported us. (George, also a Ph.D. in English and a writer himself, has graciously donated his time and talents to proofread the entire text two times.) To these loved ones and to all those striving to learn, we dedicate this book.

J.B.C., R.J.C., L.L.L.
August 8, 1993

CONTENTS

CONTENTS

CONTENTS

CONTENTS

TUTOR

A COLLABORATIVE APPROACH
TO LITERACY INSTRUCTION

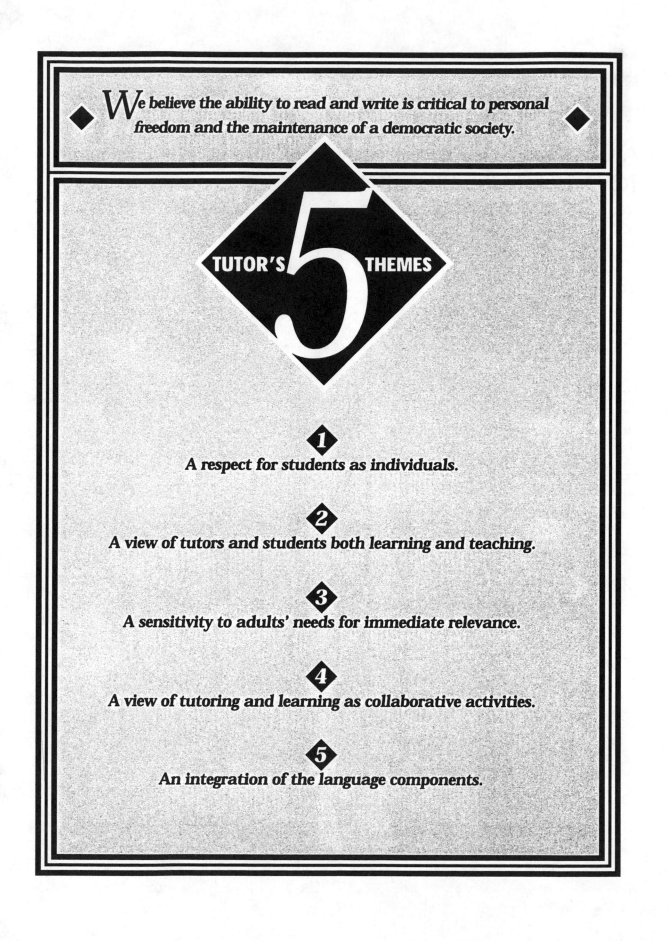

We believe the ability to read and write is critical to personal freedom and the maintenance of a democratic society.

TUTOR'S 5 THEMES

1

A respect for students as individuals.

2

A view of tutors and students both learning and teaching.

3

A sensitivity to adults' needs for immediate relevance.

4

A view of tutoring and learning as collaborative activities.

5

An integration of the language components.

INTRODUCTION

THIS BOOK IS WRITTEN FOR ALL THOSE who are willing to expend their efforts to help adults who want to become better readers and writers.

ProLiteracy America, U.S. Division of ProLiteracy Worldwide, grew out of a concern for the millions of people in the United States who cannot read and write or whose reading and writing are so inadequate that their limited literacy is a problem in their everyday lives. Some did not profit from their school experiences. Some never had opportunities to attend school regularly. Others find their reading and writing skills insufficient for the demands of this changing world. Whatever the source of their problems, millions of people need your help learning to read and write.

1

ProLiteracy America offers several trainings in tutoring basic literacy. The training in **TUTOR** is a professionally designed and field-tested workshop for the professional and non-professional reading and writing tutor. This text is designed to provide you with:

♦ A theoretical and attitudinal base from which to tutor.

♦ Demonstrations and discussions of needed skills and approaches for tutoring.

♦ Opportunities to practice these skills, which will be expanded during the training.

Interwoven throughout the text and the training are five underlying themes that you will be putting into practice as you tutor:

1. A respect for students as individuals.

2. A view of tutors and students both learning and teaching.

3. A sensitivity to adults' needs for immediate relevance.

4. A view of tutoring and learning as collaborative activities.

5. An integration of the language components.

In this text you will find professionally-accepted approaches and techniques with step-by-step instructions for tutoring basic literacy on a one-to-one basis or in a small group setting. We generally use the terms *tutors* and *students* in the plural because we are talking to all tutors about all students—whether the tutoring setting is one-to-one or in small groups.

This book reflects more than three decades of experience, both volunteer and professional, with volunteer literacy programs. Techniques in teaching reading and writing have been adapted for the use of non-professional as well as professional tutors. Workable techniques explained in **TUTOR** have emerged from a vital combination of practical experience and academically tested theory.

This text is designed to accompany ProLiteracy America's one-to-one and small group tutor training workshops, which follow a holistic, integrated approach to understanding and teaching reading and writing. The book is also designed to be used as a reference during lesson planning and tutoring.

Tutors should plan to attend additional in-service sessions provided by their local literacy programs, state literacy offices, Adult Basic Education programs, or other educational organizations in the community. Additional training is also available at ProLiteracy's annual conferences, which are open to students, tutors, trainers, administrative staff, and others interested in literacy.

This seventh version of **TUTOR** assumes that you will do a great deal of reading, writing, listening, and speaking about each topic. One of our goals, in fact, is for you to use the book as a springboard to deepen your own understanding, to explore your assumptions, and to build your knowledge of literacy and tutoring. We encourage you to write in the margins and spaces provided. Highlight important ideas; make note of those things you find helpful and those things you want to come back to later.

One word about the case studies presented in these pages: these are all accounts of actual people. We have altered names and particular details of the situations to protect the confidentiality of those involved.

We, the three authors, invite you to join us and thousands of others across the country as together we work with people who have asked for help in reading and writing. As you help others, as you touch individual lives, you too will be touched. Your life will never be the same.

◆◆◆

◆ WHAT IS LITERACY?

CHAPTER

1

WHAT IS LITERACY?

HISTORICALLY, literacy has been defined by American culture in different ways: A hundred years ago literacy meant being able to sign one's name; by World War II, being able to read at a fourth grade level; by the 1960s, having completed the eighth grade. Even today some people wish to define literacy more precisely and narrowly than others. Some place the primary emphasis on reading; some define it as "spelling," or "printing," or "sounding out words." Advanced technology and an ever-changing world have expanded the skills and strategies needed to function successfully in our world.

The National Literacy Act of 1991 defines literacy less narrowly, as "an individual's ability to read, write, and speak in English and compute and solve problems necessary to function on the job and in society, to achieve one's goals, and develop one's knowledge and potential." This definition will no doubt be refined and changed, for social and cultural influences constantly call for redefinitions of what it means to be literate.

Consider the everyday situations in which you use language to accomplish a variety of purposes. Some situations require you to receive information and make judgments; other situations demand that you express what you know to clarify your actions or involve others in the same activity. In either case you and other people are daily producers and consumers of language. The purpose of such interchanges is to understand, to communicate meanings.

INTEGRATION OF LANGUAGE COMPONENTS

People often think of literacy as only reading and writing. Based both on experience and current research, ProLiteracy America advocates that literacy instruction be viewed as involving all language components: listening, speaking, reading, and writing, as mediated through thought.

You may not ever have paid much attention to the roles of listening and speaking before now. Think about these facts:

♦ Linguists have identified about 4,000 languages. More than half of these languages do not have written forms. In many cultures reading and writing are not language components, and so are not necessary for communication.

♦ The average baby hears language equivalent to a book a day from the primary caregiver. That baby begins to talk some time in the first two years—after having heard the equivalent of 365 to 730 "novels"! At about age four, five, or six, having been able to communicate quite nicely for several years, the child in a culture having written forms of language begins to learn to read and write.

♦ Reading and writing, in our culture, are important and vital ways of communication.

RELATIONSHIPS AMONG THE LANGUAGE COMPONENTS

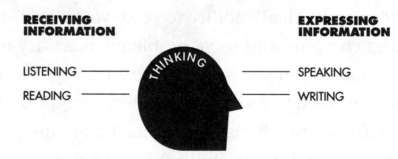

Listening and reading are two channels for receiving information; speaking and writing are two channels for expressing information. Reading and writing are communicated through written symbols; listening and speaking, through oral symbols. Reading, writing, listening, speaking—all require the individual to think, to engage in the process of expressing or receiving information.

If we separate reading from writing and listening from speaking, we simply fragment language. In short, we unnecessarily complicate matters, making language learning much more difficult than it needs to be. And if we further divide reading into a series of separate skills (sounds, vocabulary exercises, syllabification, affixes and prefixes), we continue to make reading seem less and less a part of natural language. For that reason, we present language as an integrated whole and believe that language teaching needs to integrate all the language components. This philosophy of language instruction is sometimes referred to as whole language.

REAL-LIFE LITERACY

If you cannot read Greek, this want ad will be incomprehensible to you.

ΜΑΓΕΙΡΙΣΣΑ Καλδς
Ευεφγετηματα
Απο 8 Π.Μ. εως 3 Μ.Μ.
Τηλεφωυηοατε 429–3610

This same ad in English is just as incomprehensible to a non-reader of English.

Wanted: COOK
Good Pay—Benefits
Hours: 8 am-3 pm
Call: 429-3610

Put yourself in the place of a non-reading homemaker. Imagine how frustrating it would be not to be able to read directions on a cake mix box!

EASY CAKE DIRECTIONS

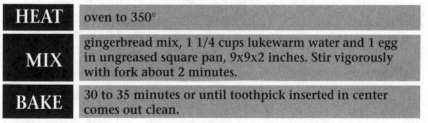

HEAT	oven to 350°
MIX	gingerbread mix, 1 1/4 cups lukewarm water and 1 egg in ungreased square pan, 9x9x2 inches. Stir vigorously with fork about 2 minutes.
BAKE	30 to 35 minutes or until toothpick inserted in center comes out clean.

Think of the things that could happen if you were not able to read signs such as these:

Suppose you were a parent with a sick child and you could not read the labels on a medicine bottle?

In each situation, literacy is a part of, not separate from, life.

Literacy helps us to remember, to organize ideas, to prove our points, to make judgments, to eat wisely, to save money, to care for our children, to improve and maintain health, to entertain ourselves, to assemble and repair products, to prepare for discussions, to broaden our views, to improve or increase efficiency at home or at work, and to be full participants in society.

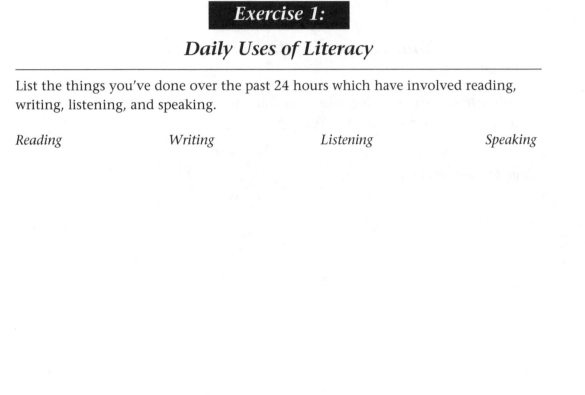

Exercise 1:

Daily Uses of Literacy

List the things you've done over the past 24 hours which have involved reading, writing, listening, and speaking.

Reading   *Writing*   *Listening*   *Speaking*

♦♦♦

Did you find it difficult to separate your daily uses of literacy into neat compartments? In any situation you listed, did you talk for five minutes, listen for five minutes, read for five minutes, study words for five minutes, spell for five minutes? You probably found that in many cases you did a little of each. In real life, "literacy" is natural and free-flowing. Rarely do any of the language components—reading, writing, listening, speaking—occur in isolation. On the contrary, language is an integrated whole.

Come back to this exercise after you've tutored for a while.

READING: ONE ASPECT OF LITERACY

Have you ever been able to "read" every single word in a passage, but when you were finished, you had no clue as to what you had just read? You found yourself merely calling words? How is it that a person can "read" but can't understand? Let's look at some definitions of reading, one aspect of literacy.

9

Exercise 2:

Your Personal Definition of Reading

Look at your own definition first. This is important because your definition of reading will determine, to a great extent, how you think reading should be taught. What comes to mind when you think of reading?

What do I do when I read?

What do I do when I see a word I can't read?

I would help someone become a reader by:

♦♦♦

PHILOSOPHY AND APPROACHES TO READING

Everyone seems to agree that the ultimate purpose of reading is to arrive at meaning. However, we can identify at least three basic views of learning to read, each of which places a different emphasis on the role of meaning. Your personal definition of reading will probably fit into one of these three broad perspectives:

◆ *View One:* Learning to read means learning to pronounce words.

◆ *View Two:* Learning to read means learning to identify words and get their meanings.

◆ *View Three:* Learning to read means learning to bring meaning to a text in order to get meaning from it. (Weaver, 1988)

As a learner-centered literacy program, ProLiteracy America subscribes to View Three.

COMPARING THE THREE VIEWS OF READING

To illustrate these three definitions, we will use the following diagram.

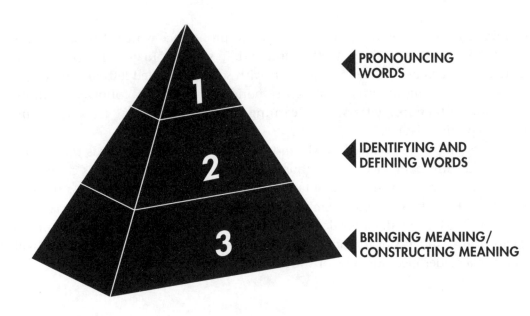

Let's examine each view.

VIEW ONE: PRONOUNCING WORDS

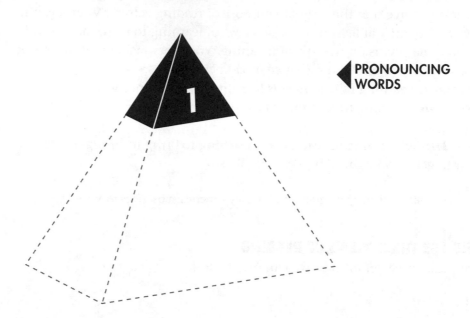

PRONOUNCING
WORDS

Learning to read, in this view, means learning to pronounce words. The basic focus is to teach students the names of letters and to train students to give the sound(s) associated with each letter. Associating letters with sounds is called letter-sound correspondence. Training in letter-sound correspondence is usually followed by more instruction in blending letters or in learning rules for combining the letters and sounds to produce words.

Words may be introduced slowly and are usually only those words that fit the letter-sound correspondences taught thus far. In some cases, lists of words comprised of the letter-sound pairings already taught are developed for the students to drill. Words from these lists are often combined into short passages.

View One is limited. Rarely do contrived passages consist of language natural to the ears of the students or the tutors. Furthermore, merely pronouncing a word will never give a reader meaning if he or she has never seen or heard the word.

Exercise 3:

An Application of View One

Suppose you suddenly found yourself able to use only the skills of View One. Suppose you could say all the words printed on a page but had no idea what they meant. To understand the limitations of View One, try the passage below:

MAS GRAN!

The gleb xupped in the middle of the zee. Jim pabbed, "Watash! I'm out of sieg!"

"Frong down, Jim," parla his esop. "The parta won't blad because we're out of sieg!"

"You're tost," pabbed Jim. "Let's tig the zee on min!"

So the two breeks tig the zee on min!

Comprehension Check:

1. What did the gleb do?
2. Where were Jim and the esop?
3. What wouldn't blad?
4. Why wouldn't it?
5. What did the two breeks do?

Skills Check:

1. What is the subject of sentence one? What is the verb?
2. What tense is *pabbed*? How do you know?
3. Make *zee* plural.
4. Make *breeks* singular.
5. Draw a line between the subject and the predicate in sentence seven.

Were you able to say all the words? Were you able to answer the questions correctly? Could you identify the parts of speech? Can you explain or retell the story? Can you define the "new" words? Suppose you knew that "zee" was a type of road and "gleb" was a particular model of car. Now re-read the passage. What a difference a context makes!

♦♦♦

VIEW TWO: IDENTIFYING AND DEFINING WORDS

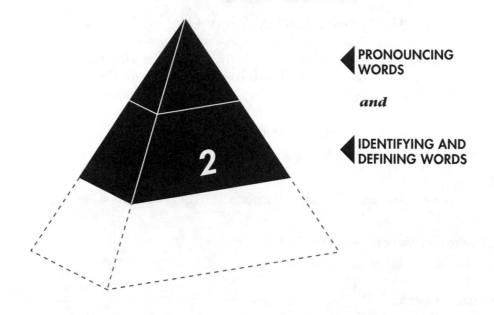

◀ PRONOUNCING WORDS

and

◀ IDENTIFYING AND DEFINING WORDS

Learning to read, in this view, means learning to identify words and understand their meaning.

The second view of reading incorporates View One, since knowing some letter-sound correspondences can be useful in identifying words. This point of view is concerned with the correct pronunciation of words paired with the ability to define them or use them in sentences. In this view, the major focus of learning to read is to build the number of words students can identify and to increase the students' collection of individual word meanings.

This view assumes that the readers' ability to say the words in print and to use those words in sentences (or to give definitions of those words) automatically leads to the building of an understanding of the material in which those words occur. It holds that the entire passage will be understood if, prior to reading, the new words for the lesson are presented.

View Two is also limited. These materials may have little or no connection to the learners' life experiences, interests, or needs. The language may be artificial, awkward, or contrived; it may not be the natural language of the students. The definitions of the words in a particular passage may not reflect the students' or a region's definition or use of them.

Exercise 4:

An Application of View Two

Read through the following list of words:

the	*centroid*	*solution*
axis	*involves*	*to*
a	*corresponding*	*of*
subject	*reference*	*placing*
table	*until*	*configuration*
magnitude	*obtaining*	*which*
inconsequential	*certain*	*correlations*
vectors	*are*	*first*
and	*process*	*residual*
through	*factor*	*considered*
adjustment	*second*	*continuing*

1. Are there words you cannot read?
2. Are there any words you cannot define?

Chances are that you can read and define all but a few of these words. You might think that you would be prepared to read these same words in the context of a written passage. Read the following:

> The centroid solution involves placing the first reference axis through the configuration of vectors; obtaining a table of residual correlations, which are subject to certain adjustments; placing the second factor through the centroid corresponding to the table of residual correlations; and continuing the process until the magnitude of the residuals can be considered inconsequential. (Source unknown.)

Would you be able to retell this passage in your own words, explaining how to use the information?

Chances are that you could not. That's not an unusual response; many readers would find it difficult. The difficulty lies not in the words or in their meanings—for we can read these words and we generally know what they mean. The difficulty lies in the very specific subject of the passage—statistics. Without a background in statistics a reader is not going to be able to make much sense of the passage.

15

Unfortunately, the ability to read words at a glance and to define these words does not ensure comprehension. This exercise should help us all recognize how frustrated adult new readers may feel when they spend weeks reviewing letters, sounds, and words in isolation with the promise of comprehension once they begin to read "real" materials. Then they pick up a menu, a magazine, the newspaper, only to find that reading those items is not like reading a word list or words out of context.

◆◆◆

VIEW THREE: BRINGING MEANING/CONSTRUCTING MEANING

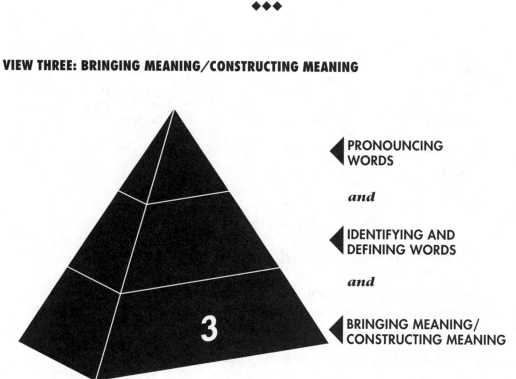

PRONOUNCING WORDS

and

IDENTIFYING AND DEFINING WORDS

and

BRINGING MEANING/ CONSTRUCTING MEANING

In View Three learning to read means learning to bring meaning to a text in order to get meaning from or to understand the text.

The primary emphasis of View Three is on building meaning, on understanding. View Two extends the original pyramid because it includes View One. By the same token, View Three creates the broad base for this same pyramid, encompassing both View One and View Two. View Three recognizes that readers use their knowledge of language and their general knowledge of the world to build personally relevant meaning from the language of the writer. This process involves the use of various strategies and skills to be presented in this book.

The difference between this third view and the first two views, however, is that in the first two reading is either an act of learning letters and sounds or a linear process of learning to recognize words and recall their meanings. In contrast, View

Three presents reading as an active, dynamic, human process that involves using all that people know about the world and their own language to make sense of new information in print. View Three incorporates Views One and Two and is the view that ProLiteracy America advocates. It underlies the approaches you will learn to use in this book.

From this view of literacy, tutoring material includes any print students need or want to read. It could be newspaper articles, ads, job announcements, manuals, personal or business letters, children's books, literature, religious material, menus, letters, the phone book, or stories the learners have written. Most importantly, material is taken from the interests and backgrounds of the students. The material is not predetermined with language made to fit a vocabulary list or the sound of a particular letter.

Since these materials are authentic or real life (e.g., a newspaper rather than a workbook designed to look like a newspaper), the resulting tutoring session is "adult." In it, people use language (read, write, talk, and listen) with real materials. Furthermore, if the tutoring material reflects a student's special interest and expertise, then that student is recognized as the expert on the topic. This may mean that while we might read words with learners, they each will be able and expected to explain to us what has been read.

This view is the most useful for a literacy tutor because it respects students' cultures and languages and validates their reasons for wanting to learn. This view allows students to be central in the process by which they learn to read.

SUMMARY

Think of the process of learning to read and write as a continuous, ongoing act expanding itself as readers/writers interact with the world of print. Print situations—where reading can occur—happen everywhere, not just in special materials written for the purpose of "teaching someone to read and write." In the same way, writing occurs in real-life, everyday situations.

We want to demonstrate to students that learning to read and write means learning to create and understand meaning. Learning to read and write is more than moving through grade levels and filling out worksheets to show mastery of the proper skills. As tutors, we all need to validate the literacy events our students engage in daily.

♦♦♦

◆ LEARNING AND TUTORING

CHAPTER

II

CHAPTER TWO:
LEARNING AND TUTORING

**A**LL HUMAN BEINGS are at one time or another both students and teachers. When it is your turn to "teach," you must respect your students as human beings fully worthy and deserving of human dignity. As tutors, you must respect students' rights to:

- Hold views different from your own.
- Have language patterns that do not match yours or the dominant culture's.
- Have goals different from the goals you might choose for them.

In essence, you want to treat students as you yourself like to be treated when the roles are reversed in life. This book uses "student" and "learner" interchangeably. The terms are not as important as the concept. The book is not, then, trying to make a social or linguistic statement when using one term or the other. All people are students and teachers, learners and facilitators, in various situations in life. Both roles require mutual respect.

HOW DO WE LEARN?

Learning is a natural human activity. We learn because we're human. It is in our nature to learn, to try to figure things out, to think, to wonder. We do it to varying degrees of success, but we all learn. What we learn, however, depends on various factors.

We learn most things in life because we are part of the demonstrations constantly going on around us. Remember the proverb:

Tell me and I will forget.

Show me and I will remember.

Let me do and I will understand.

Learning does not take place in isolation. *Literacy* learning is a collaboration between students and tutors working together as partners to reach a common goal, to complete a common task. We are all learners together, students and tutors.

Even as you tutor, you will be constantly learning. Perhaps you will learn more about how people become literate; perhaps you will learn more about the goals of your students. By assisting in the pursuit of those goals through relevant material, you might even learn about plumbing, landscaping, midwifery, or children's literature. Also, as you admit your lack of knowledge on various topics, your students may realize that they have something to teach you as well.

Students are often good problem solvers, having skills that tutors may not. Tutors can often learn about their students' abilities by listening to how they have coped with not being able to read and write in a reading and writing society. This pooling of knowledge and skills is something both will learn to do more of as tutoring sessions progress successfully.

HOW DO WE TUTOR?

Think about teaching done daily in real-life situations. Think about teaching a friend to knit or hang wallpaper, or teaching a teenager to drive a car. You don't have a book that tells you how to teach, a year's worth of lesson plans, and an outline of what is to be taught and when. So how do you do it?

You approach the students with respect. You begin by discussing the students' expectations. You provide many demonstrations. You usually show and/or tell your students what needs to be done. When it's the students' turn to "do," you usually assist, to the extent assistance is needed and welcomed, withdrawing your help if you see it is not. Then, after a while, the students do it on their own. This way, the students develop independence and responsibility, while recognizing the tutor's role as coach/facilitator. The expectation is that the students will learn what is being taught.

LEARNING AND TUTORING OF READING AND WRITING

Remember in View Three of reading the emphasis is on building meaning. This is done through the use of the learners' personal knowledge of the topic, their abilities to construct the meaning of the words in the context of the situation, and their abilities to employ various strategies including word knowledge and letter-sound correspondence as needed to understand what is being read and written.

LEARNERS AND TUTORS AS COLLABORATIVE TEAMS

Learning and tutoring take place most readily in a collaborative situation of mutual respect and shared expectations for success. As tutors, you will learn to use mutually determined goals, to negotiate what happens in a lesson, and to encourage self-assessment on your part as well as your students'.

How do adult learners look at their new tutors? What do they expect? How do new tutors feel as they meet with adult basic literacy students?

How you relate to your students as people is as important as the reading and writing learning processes you will be promoting.

WHAT IS AN ADULT LEARNER?

In the context of *TUTOR*, adult learners are those adults who need and want help in improving their proficiencies in basic reading and writing.

Exercise 5:

A New Learning Situation

Think of the factors in your own life that have helped or hindered when entering into a formal learning situation. How did you work out the details? What kind of help and encouragement did you need just to make the decision? What things discouraged you? What things encouraged you? List them in the space below:

In what ways do you think the adults you'll be working with will be similar to you? In what ways do you expect them to be different? Review this exercise after you have been tutoring for three months. Note any changes in your perceptions.

21

♦♦♦

CHARACTERISTICS OF ADULT LEARNERS

As a tutor, you should be aware of the characteristics of adult learners. You may find that you share some of these same attributes as you go through new learning experiences yourself, such as this training. No one adult tutor or student has all the characteristics listed, but reviewing them may help you be aware of them as you clarify goals and plan individual lessons.

There is no typical adult learner. Adult literacy programs have both male and female students whose ages may range from 16 to 80 plus. The student population reflects the general population. Students come from various ethnic, religious, and economic backgrounds and may represent all the possible family structures existing in the community. School experience will range from none to twelve or more years. Some may hold responsible jobs, while others are unemployed. Some have stable home lives while others are burdened with social problems. But two things are certain: they want to improve their reading and writing, and they need your help.

CREATIVITY AND ADAPTABILITY

The inability to read and write does not necessarily indicate a lack of intelligence. Many nonreaders are intelligent and creative in finding ways to compensate for the lack of proficiency in literacy. As one student commented, "I don't have trouble thinking. My trouble is just reading."

Adult students differ from children in many ways, especially in their range of life experiences. Personality, habits, attitudes, and interests have solidified to a far greater degree than in children, sometimes making adults comparatively more rigid and less receptive to change. But most adults know better what they want from educational encounters, have rich personal experiences on which to build, and can be motivated to try different approaches.

Adult learners are not blank slates. They, like all other students, have had failures. However, they also have unique talents and have had successes in some areas of life—family, church, neighborhood, or job. They simply do not have the strategies for reading and writing that they need and want. They need to be encouraged to use the adaptability and creativity they have demonstrated in other areas of their lives to develop greater proficiency with reading and writing.

APPREHENSION OR ANXIETY

Basic literacy students, like other adults going into new ventures, may very well face the experience with much hesitancy and apprehension. They may be thinking: "Am I capable of learning after all these years? Can you teach an old dog new tricks? I've failed so many times. Will this be another failure? Will my friends find out?"

Some adults do not show up for their first meeting with the tutor. Sometimes, on reflection, they decide not to go through with the lessons. Sometimes an unexpected problem arises, such as the sickness of a child. Or perhaps the problem is with transportation. There are also adults who have trouble facing new experiences; the unknown can be very frightening. It takes a great deal of courage to admit needs and to ask for assistance, and some adults cannot muster the courage to attend the first meeting.

What about you? You are the tutor. You have been trained to teach and have been told about your students in advance. Do you think you will have butterflies in your stomach when you go to your first tutoring session? Think how much more frightening this experience can be for students who have little, if any, awareness of what to expect.

UNEVEN LEARNING

Because of each adult's unique history and experience, learning cycles may be unpredictable and uneven throughout your teaching sessions.

Have you ever had a day when you could do nothing wrong, only to have it followed by a day when you could do nothing right? This up-and-down, uneven pace is natural to all learning. Some days, your students may learn quite easily, and you will feel a buoyancy about your progress. But, at other times, cues will be missed, reading will drag, and writing will just not flow. You may feel a particular student is not trying, especially if a forgetful or dull day follows a good one.

Uneven learning results from the nature of the learners and from the task itself. Don't be too upset with yourself or your learners if an occasional lesson seems unproductive. Your students may be able to do some things you think are quite complex and at the same time not be able to do things you judge as simple.

But you must be aware that many adults who come for literacy help have real learning differences. Your literacy program coordinator can help decide if those students should be referred elsewhere.

OUTSIDE RESPONSIBILITIES

Like all adults, nonreaders sometimes have problems not directly related to their inability to read and write. Some have domestic difficulties that cause them to have feelings of hopelessness. Their problems, like yours, are varied and sometimes serious. However, they must face these problems without the ease of access to information that literacy provides.

If students are disturbed by a sick child, a lost job, or domestic difficulties, they may find it difficult to concentrate on reading and writing. You cannot solve all their problems, but you can listen, ask constructive questions, and perhaps direct them to the appropriate agencies. You can also use these home situations as the source of writing and reading materials for instruction.

Many people who do not read or write are able to cope with life to their own satisfaction. They might trade off their practical skills with others who do their reading and writing for them. They are usually part of a family, neighborhood, work, or religious network and have other responsibilities to deal with in addition to attending tutoring sessions. As they increase their proficiencies with reading and writing, their place in the network often changes. These changes may be positive or they may become obstacles which will have to be dealt with.

Even time scheduled for lessons and home study may vary since all adult learners have lives with various commitments outside the literacy lessons. Most have responsibilities for the basic needs of their families, often necessitating overtime work or second jobs.

ADDITIONAL CHARACTERISTICS

Adult learners generally view themselves as responsible, self-directed, and independent, preferring to make their own decisions. They resent being treated like children and often feel threatened by formal tests. Many adult students are impatient regarding their own progress. Some will enjoy reading for pleasure and writing about their own experiences; for others, however, the most immediate needs will be for practical lessons that will satisfy their personal goals. Most adults seem to learn better in informal settings.

Of course, not all these characteristics apply to all adult learners, but being sensitive to your students' experiences and expectations will help you create a relaxed atmosphere as you plan together.

Your students may wonder what you are getting out of the tutoring experience. When they find that you are a volunteer—that you are teaching because you sincerely care and want to help—a new understanding of the collaborative tutoring partnership often results.

CHECKLIST

Characteristics of Adult Learners

Most Adult Learners:

♦ Are creative and adaptable.

♦ Are apprehensive or anxious.

♦ Learn unevenly.

♦ Have outside responsibilities beyond tutoring sessions.

♦ View themselves as responsible, self-directed, independent.

♦ Prefer to make their own decisions.

♦ Resent being treated like children.

♦ Are threatened by formal tests.

♦ Want practical lessons, satisfying personal goals.

♦ Have had varied life experiences.

WHAT MAKES AN EFFECTIVE TUTOR?

Recall a good learning experience you've had and the instructor who most positively influenced you. Reflect on the characteristics of that individual and note those qualities that still make his or her influence significant in your life.

Exercise 6:

Characteristics of My Most Memorable Instructor

List in the space below the characteristics of your most memorable instructor:

You probably have listed some of the following characteristics:

Sensitive	*Empathetic*
Patient	*Demanding*
Fair	*Humane*
Respectful	*Good-Humored*
Knowledgeable	*Prepared*
Organized	*Learner-Centered*
Flexible	

Effective teachers usually have several characteristics in common. As you begin to tutor, look for those characteristics in your own tutoring.

In the last thirty years, a great deal has been discovered about how people learn. However, good teachers, both in and out of formal school situations, have been around much longer than thirty years. Each of you probably has been fortunate enough to have had at least one person you can look to as a role model as you go through your training and into your tutoring sessions. Even though you will most likely be tutoring using approaches and techniques that differ from those you remember being taught with, aspiring to these qualities of an effective teacher/tutor will stand you in good stead.

CHARACTERISTICS OF EFFECTIVE BASIC LITERACY TUTORS

In order to be effective tutors, whether you work one-to-one or in small groups, look at the attributes of successful tutors to assess your own current strengths and needs.

The desire to help and the willingness to give time to tutoring are not enough. Learning the strategies and techniques of teaching basic reading and writing—including how to assess learners' strengths, needs, interests, and goals, and how to plan lessons based upon that ongoing assessment—is essential to effective tutoring.

Some of the skills you already have will help you to gain the new skills and strategies that you will need. Some of these are technical, the "how-to" skills, but others are based on personal qualities such as patience, understanding, and enthusiasm.

LEARNER-CENTEREDNESS

Learner-centered tutoring is directly related to the learners' needs and goals. It means keeping students at the heart of instruction and seeing students as equal partners in the learning process. Your students are entitled to know why certain techniques or strategies are important. Discussing why you are concentrating on a specific activity shows that you recognize your students' abilities to think and reason. They need to gain personal skills, not to see a demonstration of the skills you possess. The tutor must show how, not show off.

It's important for tutors to demonstrate their love and need for reading and writing. Share the reading and writing that you are doing, whether it's for pleasure, for information, or for work. Let your students know that reading and writing are lifelong skills that continue to open doors for each of us.

PATIENCE

Sometimes learning seems very slow. It takes time for everything to jell, and you might get discouraged: "What am I doing wrong? We've met for a month, and my student can't read or write." Think about yourself. Did you learn to read and write in one month? Did you quit trying because you didn't? Of course not. Expect success, keep encouraging, and above all be patient—with the learners and with yourself.

UNDERSTANDING AND RESPECT

Basic to all teaching is a respect for your students. Try to understand their situations. Most students have already faced many social problems, some of which relate to their low literacy ability. You cannot solve all their problems. You can, however, try to be understanding as you work with them.

Many students have covered up their limited skills for so long that they're often hesitant to expose their needs. Respect your students' desires for confidentiality. On the other hand, if some students want to extend themselves into new areas using their new skills, respect this and support them.

CREATIVITY

Your creativity is important. You will find yourself adapting successful techniques suggested by others, as well as ideas you've found helpful in other situations. You and your students will be directing the course of study together, based on a solid understanding of what all of you are doing.

Asking you to be creative in tutoring reading and writing would not be fair if you had no base of knowledge. *TUTOR* and the accompanying Basic Literacy Tutor Training Workshop provide the basic approaches, techniques, and knowledge about tutoring and learning that will allow you to apply your creativity. Adapt these basics to your students' needs and abilities.

SENSITIVITY

Some learners have bluffed their way along for many years, using their wits to cover up their reading and writing weaknesses. It may be very hard for these adults or teenagers to admit that they have difficulty accomplishing tasks often expected of children. Compensating behavior, like pretending to know, is hard to change, but as the relationship between you and your students develops and brings about mutual trust, these lifelong defensive habits will become less necessary. Be gentle with these learners.

A good tutor offers students clues to make success possible. Hearing "no" too often is as discouraging as being interrupted too often. If your students are puzzled or discouraged in their reading or writing, be ready to change your lesson plans. Be sensitive to your students' actions and reactions at all times.

27

Paying attention to students' problems is important in easing the tension in their lives and retaining them in the program. If you find a situation in which you feel uncomfortable or untrained, remember you are not expected to be a counselor, therapist, or social worker. You should contact your literacy program for guidance in referring that student to the appropriate agency for assistance. Dealing with problems in this way will show your concern while not asking you for skills and training you might not possess.

Be sensitive to differences in life styles, cultural backgrounds, and formal education. Remember that learning acquired in the school of life is valid and valuable. Respect your students' rich life experiences.

REALISTIC EXPECTATIONS

Sometimes tutors are unrealistic in what they think their students can accomplish. Often dreams and idealism lead to outstanding performance. But tutors must realize that some of the students with literacy problems have other problems as well. Whether it's learning differences or an unwillingness or an inability to give sessions the time and concentration needed, tutors must be realistic, aware of what their students can reasonably accomplish. Focus on what goes well and on what the students can do. Sometimes your students may have a realistic goal but an unrealistic timetable. Without an honest approach, both tutors and students can become frustrated, disillusioned, and discouraged. A blend of idealism and reality is the goal.

EMPATHY

In order to be supportive, you must empathize with your students. Let your students know that you will be supportive even when things aren't going as planned. Each of us needs to know that someone else has confidence in us and will stick with us, helping and encouraging.

SENSE OF HUMOR

A tough task is often made easier by including some light moments. Laughter often reduces tension. A good joke read or shared is a fine way to build a relationship and add pleasure to some otherwise hard work. Each instructional hour with several laughs in it will seem like a much shorter time. Tutors who can laugh at their own occasional mistakes can usually ease the tension when learners make mistakes. Be genuine, though, and beware of sarcasm. Sarcasm is always destructive.

ADAPTABILITY

People are infinitely different. Some have phenomenal memories. Some have keen intuition. Some have a knack of learning through observation. Some are plodders who will learn eventually if you have patience enough to allow them the time. Your job is to adapt your tutoring to your students' interests and abilities and to their styles of learning. Be open-minded to new ideas and a variety of teaching techniques.

ENTHUSIASM

Keep your enthusiasm high, giving genuine encouragement to your students so they will feel a sense of accomplishment with each success, no matter how small. Many small successes must occur before any long-term success can be achieved. Do not pretend success when both you and your students know it has not been attained. While excessive pressure ~~~~~~~ g are not conducive to learning, genuine respect and ~~~~~~~~~~~~~~~~~~~ h are sources of help, pride, and motivation.

ORGA

As a t ~~~~~~~~~~~~~ anning lessons and working with your students to set ~~~~~~~~~~~~~ ll never seem to be enough time for everything you ar ~~~~~~~~~~~~~ hould try to do two things.

Fi ~~~~~~~~~~~~~ on by planning between-session activities, or home p ~~~~~~~~~ give your students practice in both reading and writing. Second, focus your sessions on the purpose of the lesson.

You are responsible for working with your learners, showing up on time, observing and assessing how they are doing, planning the lessons, demonstrating/modeling, encouraging, maintaining records, and reporting to your literacy office. Because your main job is to help your students grow in reading, writing, and comprehension skills, each session with your students must be a tutoring session.

You need to pay special attention to your conversation. Of course you want to be friendly and personable with your students, but small talk shouldn't interfere with the purpose of the lesson. In addition, some adults may use chatty conversation to avoid the task because they feel unprepared or anxious. You may suggest that you use the first five minutes or perhaps the last minutes to catch up on personal conversation; at the same time you will have to decide when a listening friend is needed. Use your own good judgment.

COMMITMENT

Success stories are encouraging, but not all students will be successful. Teenage and adult nonreaders are on the lower steps of a ladder, and that next step up is often very big. Some may never take it. Working with their own tutors is often the last hope for many adults. You are encouraged not to give up before you have abundant evidence that there will not be enough progress to sustain the gains in proficiency. Check with your program coordinator to see if a focus on survival skills for a short period of time would be appropriate.

As you move to help someone learn to read and write better, remember that positive personal qualities and knowledge about learning and tutoring are needed. The fact that you have chosen to try to help someone shows that you are motivated.

Personal Characteristics of Effective Tutors

◆ Learner-Centeredness

◆ Patience

◆ Understanding and Respect

◆ Creativity

◆ Sensitivity

◆ Realistic Expectations

◆ Empathy

◆ Sense of Humor

◆ Adaptability

◆ Enthusiasm

◆ Organizational Skills

◆ Commitment

DYNAMICS OF COLLABORATIVE TUTORING SESSIONS

The process of collaborative tutoring is the same whether you are teaching one-to-one or in a small group of three to five. You are a team or partnership of people working together to accomplish the same goal. The structure, elements, or steps of the collaborative session are also the same. The differences in the two situations are in the interactions either between two people or among a group of people. As you work with your student or small group, you might want to anticipate the stages of development.

CHANGING RELATIONSHIPS

The relationship between two people or among the members of a small group changes with time as they work together. These stages of change are somewhat predictable, and understanding them can be helpful to adjusting your style and role to support success in learning.

The following discussion of the stages through which a one-to-one or small group relationship progresses is based on the work of B. W. Tuckman and M. A. C. Jensen (1977).

TUCKMAN'S MODEL OF GROUP PROCESS

STAGES	CHARACTERISTICS	TUTOR'S ROLE	ISSUES

FORMING	Getting Acquainted
	Tentative Behavior
	"What's in it for me?"
	Testing
	"Will I fit in?"
		Leader
		"Carries the Ball"
		Clearly Delineates
		  Objectives and
		  Expectations
		Accepting of
		  "Teacher" Focus
		Supporting Interpersonal
		  Relationships
			Dependence
			Fear of Unknown
			Trust
			Looking for Authority
			  Figure
			Need for Security

STORMING	Conflict
	Frustration
	Expressions of Emotion
	Growing Independence of
	  Individual Group
	  Members
	Volatile
	Increase in Student-to-
	  Student Interactions
		Conflict Manager
		Acceptance of the Impor-
		  tance of Conflict
		Support
		Encouragement
		Attention to Student's
		  Concerns
			Challenge to Leadership
			Need to Belong
			Need for Social Interaction
			Need to Assert
			  Individuality

NORMING	Cooperation
	Team Spirit
	Expressions of Opinions
	Group Unity
	Shared Responsibility
	Group Decision Making
		Guider
		Promoting Democratic
		  Procedures
		Enabling People to Take
		  on Leadership
			Group Cohesion

PERFORMING	Productivity
	Problem-Solving
	Interdependence
	Maturity
		Resource
		Minimum Supervision
		Occasional Reinforcement
		  for Outstanding
		  Achievement
		Facilitator
			Participatory
			  Democracy
			Team Work
			Getting the Job Done

ADJOURNING	Re-emergence of
	  Earlier Issue
	Sadness
	Celebratory
		Facilitator
		Celebrator
		Sometimes a Guider
		Acceptance of Feelings
			Resistance to Ending
			Grieving
			Affirming the Group's
			  Achievements
			Closure

The stages suggested are in order: forming, storming, norming, performing, and adjourning.

FORMING

The initial stage of a team's development provides the orientation to its purpose and procedures. Initially the team consists of two or more individuals who bring with them a set of experiences that have shaped them to act in certain ways in groups. These sets of behaviors may or may not be compatible.

Because this is a new situation, there are bound to be anxieties. The members do have a common goal—to be successful in working together. In this case, their goal is to help the students improve reading and writing skills. They may not be quite sure what to expect, how they can contribute, or how they can benefit.

The tutor takes an active role as leader in the forming stage, identifying goals, setting lesson plans, and planning sessions. It is essential that the tutor facilitate the process of getting acquainted. The tutor's attention to detail in the forming stage provides the sense of security that allows the students to take risks. Trust is crucial if learning is to take place.

In the forming stage, students generally expect their tutors to direct the next stages, to plan the lessons, and to take the lead in goal setting as well as setting up the rules. It takes time for learners to trust their tutors in other than leadership roles.

STORMING

At this stage, team members often express emotion and sometimes disagree on issues. The process of storming involves passage from the dependence of the students in the forming stage to a growing independence and sometimes a resistance to formal leadership. Open disagreement is normal, healthy, and necessary if a group is to grow. The way problems are managed will determine whether the learning experience will be positive.

There will be clear indications that the students are ready for more responsibility, perhaps by their assuming some of the leadership roles. The tutor may have to deal with his or her own desire to be in total control, but must be willing to give up the total role of directive leader, or team development may suffer. The tutor provides direction and structure for the lessons, but more effort is placed on clarifying and explaining the rationale behind the reading and writing tasks.

You are probably tutoring in a way new to the learners. You are insisting that each student take responsibility for his or her own learning. You are working to shift this responsibility from yourself to the students. This transfer of authority is sometimes difficult. It is often hard for tutors to give up the authority as well as for students to assume it.

If learners in one-to-one situations become upset, directing energy toward discussing and writing about what can be done will often help provide a practical way for them to gain practice in directing their own learning. In a small group setting, as students feel more comfortable with their tutors and more secure about themselves, they often are more willing to assert themselves by expressing personal opinions.

They may question the value of some of the techniques and materials. This shows an element of growth, that they are ready for more responsibility, for more leadership in setting their own goals.

NORMING

The norming stage is characterized by a growing sense of cooperation. There is more expression of opinion and a greater sense of unity. Individual personalities emerge, and decision-making by the learners is increasingly evident. There is less dependence on the tutor for guidance.

The tutor's job at this stage can be more demanding. A balance must be struck between the students taking over some leadership functions (presenting, explaining, summarizing, suggesting or setting lesson objectives and reading materials) and the tutor retaining enough leadership functions so that the learning won't get bogged down in frustration and failure. The process of sharing leadership and accepting comfortable norms is crucial. The tutor must support the team feeling that is necessary for self-directed learning.

Generally, students show an increased desire for action, making it possible for the team to accomplish a good deal. Because there is often a surge of productivity, the tutor's tendency might be to push hard on reading and writing tasks. The tutor must be careful to avoid slipping back into a directive leadership role. Shared leadership will draw this team forward into maturity and productivity.

Learners and tutors have developed their relationships with each other enough to trust and to know that their ideas and emotions will be accepted, and they are free to work on the tasks ahead. There probably will be more "give and take" as each student takes on more responsibility.

PERFORMING

The performing stage is characterized by productivity and maturity. Tutors and students are more accepting of individual differences. The process of learning and planning becomes the responsibility of students as well as tutors. Plans are tested through discussion, and reading materials and lessons have more relevance to real-life situations.

People in both the one-to-one and small group situations can relax. Listening skills have been developed by both tutors and students. There is a real sense of accomplishment and satisfaction as the task of improving reading and writing becomes more and more a reality.

Students depend less and less on the tutor. Each learner has become more competent and more self confident, exhibiting a higher degree of motivation. Many leadership functions are assumed by the students.

ADJOURNING

Eventually the tutoring team must come to an end. Adjourning should not be done abruptly. It should allow time for affirmations, for sadness at parting, and for closure.

The tutor may take a more active role, particularly as a guide, encouraging an acceptance of the grieving, and facilitating the team through celebrations and affirmations. The tutor may want to guide the learners toward celebrating each one's progress. Perhaps you could suggest that your student share a poem or a reading at your affiliate's annual student/tutor meeting. In a small group, each student could be highlighted for one lesson with stories, poems, or presentations written and read by fellow group members. You may want to focus on the next step in your students' continuing education.

Because the students have been actively involved in all parts of the lessons, they may want to plan a closing event. It may be as simple as meeting for coffee and doughnuts or lunch, or perhaps a picnic to include both the tutor's and students' families. Many students can accept a disbanding of their lessons more easily if they know they can continue to call the tutor for encouragement, for direction, or perhaps just to "touch base" again.

LEADERSHIP STYLE

If the tutor's leadership style is mismatched with the learner's stage of development, problems can occur. Most people are comfortable with a particular style of leadership and have developed their skills in only specific ways. Adherence to a particular style of leadership will limit the tutor's effectiveness and the student's or the group's chance for success.

Tutors willing to examine their leadership styles and to adjust to the needs of the learners will provide a much more positive learning experience. They will also increase the probability of the students' improving their reading and writing.

As a tutor you will want to structure the learning situation in such a way that each learner is always a participant, whether working one-to-one or in a small group. Your role will change at each stage of your tutoring cycle as you help each student move to become independent and self-directed, to be able to most fully direct and be responsible for his or her own learning.

ONGOING INFLUENCES

Although you and your students might not always achieve success together, you may never know how far the ripples go from the pebble you drop into the pond. You may never know how much influence you may have when you meet with your students. Sometimes you may seem to fail with a student, but underneath that "failure" may be success in a different form.

For example, one literacy program dropout felt that he had failed in everything and sought solace in alcohol. But he insisted that his teenage son stay in school, that he not become a dropout like his father. The hope of learning was not strong enough to sustain the father, but the glimpse of the skills he might have had strengthened this man's concern for his son.

On the other hand, you may be teaching a potential leader. Leaders sometimes come from unlikely places. As a volunteer, you can have profound effects on the lives you touch.

In the world of finance, investment counselors use the phrase "growth potential." Consider that phrase as you tutor. It is possible that through your work and influence with a parent the attitude of a whole family could change. The children may begin to look at their parents with new respect, regarding their own learning as being more important than they had realized. With learning as a central focus for both children and parents, the whole idea of staying in school and completing an education takes on new meaning.

As you work with students from different backgrounds, you'll never know whether they or their children might become leaders or influence someone else destined for leadership. This is a growth potential with possibilities that extend far beyond your instruction.

Your constant reassurance is needed. Good tutors encourage their students to take responsibility for their own learning, letting them know that home study and practice are a real part of each session. The habits of reading and writing must be exercised every day, not only to progress but also to keep from losing these skills.

Volunteers, whether tutors or students, readers or nonreaders, need support and encouragement to get involved in other aspects of learning. Be sure that you, as a tutor, both get and give support. Look to your program and other training opportunities for continuing in-service training and support.

♦♦♦

◆ READING

CHAPTER

III

READING

STUDENTS can gain confidence and practice in understanding or building meaning during their reading if they are aware of and consciously try to do what many good readers do when they read. Proficient readers instinctively have a kind of dialogue with a text before, during, and after reading.

Before reading, good readers usually examine the text, make predictions about the nature of the reading, flip through the pages to see the format and the illustrations, make sure it looks like something they'd like to read.

During reading, good readers talk to themselves, making sure they understand what they've been reading, summarizing key ideas if they're reading more difficult material, rereading if they find they're not understanding. They also check to see if their predictions were accurate; they update those predictions as they read further along in the text. This "self-talk" can be silent or aloud, but it allows readers the opportunity to check their understanding.

Sometimes good readers take notes; sometimes they go to the dictionary. They often quickly skim non-technical material. Proficient readers vary the strategies they use when they read depending on the difficulty of the text and their interest in and knowledge about the subject.

After reading, good readers usually "respond" to the material. After reading fiction, poetry, or inspirational essays, readers often respond emotionally: "I loved the ending." "I can't believe it ended that way." "Margaret was such an admirable character." "I wish that story had not ended." After the emotional response good readers are ready to look at other aspects of the text: "What did I learn?" "Did any of my predictions prove true?" "How does it compare with something else I've read or with my experience?" "What were the new words?"

INTRODUCING READING STRATEGIES

Readers are generally not aware of these strategies. You can work to help new readers understand why strategies are important and help them incorporate this kind of self-talk into their own reading. Below are guidelines to help you translate these strategies to your students as you tutor.

BEFORE READING:

1. Get students into the habit of previewing and predicting. Have students look at the title, chapter headings, subheadings, bold type, and illustrations before reading the text. Through these activities, they are making connections in their minds between the subject of the material and what they already know. They should also be asked to predict what they think the passage will be about. Remember, you are working with adults and need to recognize the rich background knowledge and experience many bring.

2. If the material has a summary, have students read it first and retell it to you in their own words. If students cannot paraphrase (retell the story or information read in their own words), suggest that you or the students read the summary one more time and try again. If students still cannot paraphrase, you do the paraphrasing as a model and proceed.

3. Help students to identify the type of text. Is it a poem, essay, story, technical manual, job application form? Knowing the type of text will help students make predictions and identify purposes for reading.

4. Help students identify the purpose for reading. Are they reading for pleasure, for information, for instruction, to pass a test, to be inspired? Their purpose for reading will have direct impact on which strategies to use during reading.

DURING READING:

1. Encourage students to check constantly for meaning. They need to be asking themselves, "Does this make sense?" Your purpose here is to encourage active reading, a kind of dialogue between readers and their text. This is the time to check predictions and make new ones.

2. In reading silently, when students come to a word they don't know, suggest they skip the word and read on. Usually the meaning will come through the context.

3. In reading aloud, when students come to a word they stumble over, supply the word quietly and allow them to read on.

4. Help students read in phrases rather than word by word. You may need to model this procedure.

AFTER READING:

1. Allow for the emotional response if it's appropriate to the type of reading you've been doing. You can do this easily by asking, "What did you think about . . . ?"

2. Ask students to summarize the reading by talking or writing. (If the reading material describes a process the students need to repeat, ask the students to describe the process step-by-step.)

3. If the reading is an opinion piece, ask the students to restate the writer's opinion and then to agree or disagree with the opinions expressed in the reading. Your main questions will be "What is the author's view?" and "Do you agree with the author? Why or why not?"

4. If students want to master the material for a test, ask them to recall what they need to remember. You or the students can make notes or lists to keep for review or future reference.

5. If students like to keep records of new words they are learning, ask them to recall or look back to find new words from the lesson.

Helping students learn to use strategies before, during, and after their reading will improve their comprehension because it makes them aware of the active nature of the reading process.

COMPREHENSION

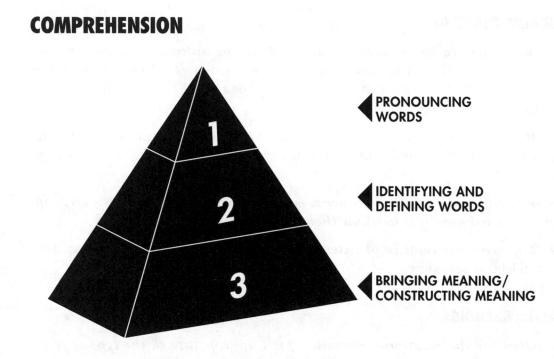

1

2

3

◀ PRONOUNCING
WORDS

◀ IDENTIFYING AND
DEFINING WORDS

◀ BRINGING MEANING/
CONSTRUCTING MEANING

In the Three Views of Reading pyramid, comprehension or construction of personal meaning is the base. As you work with students, the emphasis of each lesson should be to make sense of what is read. To help attain that goal, you can introduce other strategies. However, these strategies should be seen as stepping stones to the primary goal of making sense of the text.

LITERAL INTERPRETATION

The literal meaning of a passage is the meaning of the words on the page. Literal interpretation does not include students' feelings or opinions. An easy check for literal meaning is to ask students to retell in their own words what they read. If this is difficult for them, you could ask such questions as "What was the story about?" or "What happened at the end?"

If students cannot retell the story, you will want to know whether the problem is one of too much material or if there is some skill lacking that prevents retelling. To see if the problem is too much material, reduce the quantity by having them read just one paragraph. If they cannot retell what the paragraph is about, deal with a single sentence or two. If this is still not successful, break the sentence into phrases by putting slash marks in pencil after words that should be read together:

Every payday / we save some money / and we put it / in the bank.

Now paraphrase this sentence for the students, modeling how to retell. Then use another sentence, suggesting that the students do the retelling.

This practice will provide a basis for literal comprehension of the words of the author. Literal comprehension can occur only if the readers' personal experiences are varied enough to contain similar ideas.

For some readers, the ideas and concepts, not the words, are out of the realm of their understanding or experiences. If you find such a situation with your students, work on vocabulary to extend experiences by providing pictures, explanations, or demonstrations.

INFERENCE

When you are sure the students understand the facts the author has presented, you can ask for responses requiring higher level comprehension skills. From the stated information, you can ask students to make inferences (i.e., draw logical conclusions) about ideas not fully expressed or developed in the text.

For example, suppose students read this sentence:

> As soon as Congress adjourns, senators leave Washington behind and head
> for home.

They might conclude that Washington is not the senators' home and perhaps is not their favorite place.

Consider this sentence:

> He froze in his tracks as he heard the squeak again from the dark corner.

You could ask the students what the expression "to freeze in his tracks" means. Did he literally turn to ice? You will want the students to realize that the expression refers to emotion, not to temperature, and that tracks have something to do with stopping his motion, not with trains or jogging.

Our language is metaphorical. Our words have multiple levels of meaning. In addition, various communities have their own expressions that are not understandable to other communities.

Another simple way to introduce the multiple levels of meaning in a passage is to use proverbs, fables, or parables. Having read Aesop's fable about a fox, you could discuss the literal meaning ("There was a fox . . .") and then the various interpretive meanings ("What do you think Aesop was trying to tell us?").

How do we all acquire the knowledge to be able to make inferences? It comes from a vast reservoir of information collected over a lifetime. There is no specified way to assure this information base. However, the more we read, listen, and experience, the more we encounter a rich variety of words and expressions, and the greater is our capacity to understand the next idea that comes along.

From the oral language base, we proceed to recognize words in print that represent ideas or meaning. From these perceived meanings and our own inner storehouse of information, we think beyond the words of the text in response to our own experiences. We check out the validity of such thoughts by determining if they are consistent with what we already know. Then we feel justified to arrive at certain conclusions. When we receive and interpret the initial data from print sources, we call it reading.

CRITICAL THINKING

Often people who have grown to adulthood without being able to read have such a reverence for the printed page that they accept everything in print as the absolute truth. Help students question the authority of authors when they read materials open to interpretation (e.g., newspapers, self-help books, opinion articles).

The first step is to show students the difference between facts and opinions. Good news reporting should present the facts, but the editorial page is a collection of opinions. Advice columnists give their own opinions about people's problems. Give students practice in raising questions when opinions are stated:

"What evidence does this writer give us?"

"Does the evidence relate to the question or does it seem off the subject?"

"How did the writer collect his evidence? Who exactly does he say he interviewed?"

"Is he an expert? What do other experts say?"

"Can we check this for ourselves?"

Acquaint your students with the usual persuasion devices used in advertising or in political speeches.

PROPAGANDA STRATEGIES:

Plain folks device: "I'm just a poor country boy myself."

Band wagon technique: "Everybody agrees . . . . "

Appeal to authority: "Men of distinction smoke . . . . "

Name calling to avoid the issues: "My opponent is a card-carrying . . . . "

You might enjoy working on listening and speaking experiences with your students. Here are a few suggestions. Tape political advertisements or political debates. Look at advertisements and editorials in magazines or on television. Analyze them critically: What is actually being said? Is the claim too good to be true? Proceed cautiously if you need to. Remember the old adage about not discussing sex, religion, or politics. If you don't think you or your students can discuss these issues critically without falling into arguments, skip politics and go on to advertising.

Tutors work with literal and inferential comprehension and critical thinking skills not only to help students in their literacy lessons but also in their lives. Use the following questioning strategies to help students.

DIRECTED QUESTIONING STRATEGIES

Reading opens doorways to thinking. Encourage your students to think of the *who*, *what*, *when*, *where*, *why*, and *how* when they are reading and writing. You can help learners clarify their thoughts for reading and writing through questioning:

1. Use questions to encourage discussion about events, opinions, and procedures in the reading material:

    Who would you say is the most important character? Why?

2. Ask questions that will structure students' answers in concise and logical order:

    Yes, I agree that the main character seemed to overreact to his partner. But what happened first?

3. Ask questions that will lead students to speculate or read between the lines:

    Why did so few supplies reach the people who needed them? What do you think the author wants us to think about that government?

4. Try to avoid questions that require only a yes/no response:

    What did you think about this book?

   rather than

    Did you like this book?

5. Ask students to formulate questions. This may be difficult for them at first, but after you've modeled some questions, they'll probably follow your lead. Encourage students to ask themselves these questions as they read.

FLUENCY IN READING

Many new readers are hesitant to read aloud. Often it's because previous experiences have been negative. They have had little practice and know their reading aloud just doesn't flow smoothly. They're embarrassed. However, hearing your students read aloud can provide you with information on their comprehension and word attack strategies. Except during a formal assessment task, suggest that students read silently before reading aloud. Don't hesitate to have them reread the passage several times until they feel comfortable with the material.

As students come to words they stumble over, quietly supply the words and allow them to continue. When students have to wrestle with individual words, they become so busy concentrating on a particular word that they often lose sight of the meaning of the sentence or paragraph. To avoid interfering with the flow of the material, merely supply the word and move on.

Here are some ways to help students develop fluency.

MODELED READING

Increase students' fluency in reading aloud by modeling, letting them hear how reading flows in phrases, like spoken language. Spend ten minutes or so at the end of each lesson reading to your students. Don't ask comprehension questions afterward. Just let them enjoy and reflect.

ASSISTED READING

SILENT READING FOLLOWING A LEADER

Another effective exercise to help students' reading is to give them copies of material to be read and suggest that they follow the words and read silently as you read aloud or play a tape. As they gain confidence in reading aloud, ask individual students to read aloud as you and/or other students follow their reading.

CHORAL READING

It's helpful to you and to the students—whether in one-to-one or small groups—to read aloud together. Have copies of the same reading material, so that each of you can follow the reading. Some students may join in softly at first, not sure of their reading. You set the pace, reading slowly enough for them to keep up but fast enough not to distort the meaning. A joint effort that doesn't point out any individual student's weaknesses, choral reading can be a learning experience that builds self-confidence.

Home practice in choral reading could include asking students to read material in print and on tapes. They can get the rhythm of reading aloud by reading with good readers even on tapes.

IMPRESS OR SHADOW READING

This exercise can follow the choral reading. Tell students that you will all read together, but that you will gradually fade out, or fade in, allowing the individual or small group to take leadership. You might want the students to run their index fingers under the words in their copies of the text as they're reading, keeping the pace set even if occasional "errors" are made. As students become proficient with a selection, reduce the volume of your own voice and gradually become silent. But continue the finger movements under the words so that the students maintain the pace.

You can get the feel of how much reinforcement is needed, gradually lowering your voice to give them confidence that they can read aloud fluently.

PHRASE READING

The degree to which learners can be fluent in reading may well determine the degree to which they comprehend reading material. As you introduce material to students, read it in units of meaning (phrases, clauses, sentences). Intonation patterns in your oral reading will provide students with additional "clues" for comprehension.

For learners who are reading word-by-word, block off phrases in the materials being used:

Most work / is done well / when people are happy / and know their jobs.

Use reading material within the students' reading abilities. The goal is that students recognize how reading flows in phrases.

SUMMARY

Comprehension is the basis of literacy, of reading and writing, of listening and speaking. As a tutor, you need to know when comprehension is taking place and how to help students help themselves as they learn to use comprehension strategies. Success means students become more self-directed and independent as they search for information and construct meaning.

♦♦♦

◆ TECHNIQUES USED IN COLLABORATIVE TUTORING

CHAPTER

IV

TECHNIQUES USED IN COLLABORATIVE TUTORING

A COLLABORATIVE APPROACH consists of two or more people working together as partners toward a common goal. How can collaboration be applied and adapted to tutoring both in a one-to-one and a small group setting?

In any situation, remember the five themes, knowing they apply to both one-to-one and small group situations:

1. A respect for students as individuals.
2. A view of tutors and students both learning and teaching.
3. A sensitivity to adults' needs for immediate relevance.
4. A view of tutoring and learning as collaborative activities.
5. An integration of the language components.

Your responsibility is to see that individual needs are addressed. We would like to share some effective techniques for you to use for developing certain skills within your tutoring situation. It is important for you to be comfortable with a variety of techniques in order to plan learner-centered lessons.

In this chapter you will be introduced to the following basic ways to help your students develop or extend proficiency with reading and writing:

- ◆ Language Experience.

- ◆ Sight Words and Context Clues.

- ◆ Phonics.

- ◆ Word Patterns.

When you learn how to use and adapt these techniques, you will be able to incorporate them into your lessons as indicated by your assessment of students' particular needs.

Every lesson will not necessarily include all of these techniques. In fact, you will recognize that many students will not need to work with some of these techniques. Remember the adult learners' needs for immediate relevance as you select the most appropriate techniques for them. Also, bear in mind that the language components are integrated; therefore, it is not recommended that any lesson be spent on repeated drills of isolated components or "fragmented subskills."

As you read this chapter, recognize that some techniques are isolated for the purpose of discussion and explanation. However, it is not recommended that techniques be emphasized in isolation. Rather, if you feel your students would benefit from seeing how a word pattern (or some other technique) may make other words more predictable, you should address that through a prominent pattern in the material being read or written by the students. This is, of course, more relevant to the students than selecting a pattern (e.g., -*ack*) for drill on worksheets. Remember to select your teaching strategies but weigh your choices against the five themes that pervade this book.

LANGUAGE EXPERIENCE

An important element of this tutoring process is language experience. *Language experience* is a story or experience dictated by students and written by the tutor. Using both the learners' own experiences and language as the basis for instructional material is an effective way of collaborating with learners from the very first lesson. This approach gives immediate success and is an ice-breaker in a new teaching situation. It also gives you insights into the learners' worlds that can be of great help in selecting materials for a series of lessons.

In language experience, the emphasis is on demonstrating the connections between thought and oral language as written language through dictation. Language experience can be used with those students whose experiences with writing are so severely limited or negative that they need continued demonstrations of the connections between their thoughts and written language. This technique allows even beginning readers to create sophisticated oral compositions which they can easily produce. Language experience also works well with any level of group-composing in which one person writes as the others talk.

To see one's own words written down provides the best of all possible motivations, for it is an individual's own story. The experience story is an expression in each learner's own words of:

◆ A personal experience.

◆ A procedure from work.

◆ Material which has been read to the learner.

◆ Anything else of interest to the learner.

STEPS IN USING THE LANGUAGE EXPERIENCE APPROACH

1. Converse to identify an experience or topic.

Invite your students to talk. If students are hesitant or reluctant to talk, take the initiative. Read a few paragraphs from a newspaper or magazine article that you think the students will find interesting. Show a picture from a newspaper or a book and ask what is happening.

Quiet and sympathetic listening will be necessary as you discover the interests and concerns of your students. Learners may need time for thoughtful reflection. Ask leading questions, but do not pressure. Give periods of silence: signs of thoughtful reflection in preparation for speaking should signal silence from you. However, extended periods of silence accompanied by signs of restlessness and embarrassment should prompt you to speak, perhaps rephrasing a question or statement that your students may not have understood.

2. Record the students' words.

When working with a single student, it is simple to record the student's words. You may wish to use a sheet of carbon paper so that you'll have a copy for your own file. For ease of recognition, use the manuscript writing style shown on page 163 as a model. Neatly print the words your student says. If the student talks faster than you can write, ask to have a sentence repeated. Your student will enjoy this. If using the computer, type the words so you and the student can see them on the screen. When teaching a beginning reader, keep the first dictated story as short as possible.

Similarly, with several students in a small group, write on the board or on paper the words the group has decided on. A leader who speaks generally for the group may emerge, but encourage participation by all.

If your students can write even in a limited way, encourage them to write at least a short language experience. If they are reluctant to write, offer to take dictation in these first attempts.

Do not call attention to your students' English usage in early lessons. If the dictation is "Me and my wife . . ." or "We sure does . . ." write it exactly that way. If it is simply a mispronunciation or a dialect different from standard English, such as the word *ax* for *ask*, write the word conventionally.

Later, as you work with your students, you may find that they want help with grammar and usage. That is the time to make suggested changes.

Many dialects eliminate or modify the middle and final sounds in words. For example, the word *floor* is often pronounced as if it were spelled *flo* in some language communities. In another community, natives say "Pahk y'cah" (Park your car), also omitting the *r* sound. It is important not to regard such modifications as incorrect. You may not realize how often you modify a letter-sound relationship in the middle of words. We hear countless examples of such modifications every day. Every speaker speaks a dialect just as every speaker speaks with an accent. Don't stress these dialectical differences.

3. Read the story.

Make sure your students are able to see the page or the board on which you have written, as you say "Here's what you said. Watch and listen carefully while I read it to you. Is this the way you want it written?" Read the entire message. If you are at a computer, you can read from the screen or print copies for yourself and each student. Point to each word as you read. When pointing, be sure to use a pencil, ruler, or one finger as a pointer. Do not point with your whole hand because the learners will not know which finger is the pointer. Say the words naturally in meaningful groups even though you are going slowly. Avoid "word calling" or saying each word separately.

Reread the first sentence, pointing to each word as you read it. Then ask the learners to read the sentence with you as you or your students slide a finger under the words. This may take a little encouragement for shy students, especially those who can't read at all. You could remind them that they already know what the sentence says because these are their own words. Feel free to tell them words they're stuck on. Read the sentence again with your students until they seem more confident. Make the reading challenging but not painful.

If learning proceeds slowly, concentrate on one sentence. If your students learn more quickly, use as much of the story as they can absorb. Reading more than one sentence at a time will help keep the meaning of the whole passage in mind. This attention to meaning helps build both comprehension and fluent reading.

4. Ask students to select meaningful words.

Help your students read some of the words from their stories out of context (that is, separate from the stories).

The following story could have been told by one student or by several:

We got new jobs. It's packing bags at the supermarket. You got to put things in a
bag just so or you'll bust them. We get tired, but we like the pay.

Have the students choose three or four meaningful words from the story that
they want to learn first. Underline each of these words in the story and copy each
word on a word card. Encourage students to write their own word cards as soon as
possible.

| jobs | supermarket | tired | pay |

In the above story the words *jobs, supermarket, tired,* and *pay* might have been
the meaningful words that were chosen to be learned first.

5. Teach each selected word.

Ask the students to look at each word card carefully. Say the word as written,
asking the students to repeat the word. Ask the students to place each word card under its duplicate in the story, reading the word as matching takes place. Then ask the
students to mix up the cards and ask the students to read each word again, referring
to the story if necessary.

Make another set of word cards for your own file, placing them in a box as a
"word bank" for use in writing, spelling, and quick practicing or as a source of review. Maintaining a complete set of words learned shows your students their steady
progress.

6. Reread the story.

Ask students to reread the story with you. Be sure to read in meaningful phrases
or sentences. You may want to ask students to reread the story on their own if you
think they are ready. By rereading the story you are returning the individual words
you've been working on back to their context, the story. Rereading also provides
learners with the opportunity to read for meaning.

7. Give students a copy of the story and word cards.

If you have one student, give him or her the original copy of the story along
with the word cards to take home for reading practice. If there are several students,
suggest that they copy the story, or give them one of the carbon copies or copies
from a copy machine or printer. You might suggest they think of other words that
they want to learn from the story and make word cards for these words.

Your students can progress from dictating simple stories to being responsible
for writing them later. What is important at this stage is to see their own spoken
words in written form.

EXAMPLES OF STUDENT STORIES

Experience stories, like the following examples, can lead to learning other skills as well.

One learner told his tutor how he drove from Syracuse, New York, to Clarksdale, Mississippi. The tutor got a map and discussed *north*, *south*, *east*, and *west*. Together they planned a variety of possible trips, with the learner giving the directions. It was fun to do and he learned quickly. He dictated the following experience story:

> I live in Syracuse. I was born in Clarksdale, Mississippi. I want to go down
> there by car. I go south to Pennsylvania, south and west to Cleveland, Ohio,
> south and west to Louisville, Kentucky, south to Memphis, Tennessee, and south
> to Clarksdale, Mississippi.

This led to his realizing the need to read road signs and to his next project of word cards with road signs.

Another learner, Bob Jamieson, worked as a handyman in the maintenance department of a local factory. Because his reading was at a beginning level, he knew which bottles to use only by associating colors with the materials. He is now learning to read the words on the bottles, incorporating them into his experience story. Reading in this way is a practical help on the job:

> First I use a dust mop and mop the floor. Then I use other things:
> Floor Dressing (light brown)
> Disinfectant (dark green)
> Floor Soap (pink)
> Wax (white)
> Ammonia (clear like water)

A third learner, Maxine Fielding, had legal problems. She wanted to write to a lawyer, but she had little confidence in her ability to do this because her reading and writing were at a low level. She began to solve her problem by dictating a letter to her tutor which she learned to read and later copied:

> Dear Mr. J.
>
> I'm writing this letter to inquire about your assistance. The police arrested me
> on a charge of burglary. I was walking down the street when I heard a noise in
> a store. So I went to see what was going on. When I went in I saw two young
> boys climbing out a window in the back of the store. I explained to the police,
> but they don't believe me. Can you defend me?
>
> Yours truly,
>
> Maxine Fielding

CHECKLIST ✔

Language Experience

1. Identify an experience or topic through conversation.

2. Record students' words exactly as spoken.

3. Read the story, asking the students to read the story after you.

4. Ask the students to select meaningful words, underlining those words and putting them on individual word cards.

5. Teach each selected word. Ask the students to shuffle the word cards and read them, referring to the story if necessary.

6. Reread the story together. Ask the students to reread the story.

7. Give a copy of the story and word cards to the students for home study, keeping a copy for yourself.

As your students progress and can read more of the words they dictate in their stories, you might want to teach only those words that they cannot read.

When you and your students have developed a text using the language experience approach, you may use it as a basis for the following techniques.

SIGHT WORDS AND CONTEXT CLUES

A sight vocabulary is a stock of words immediately recognized and understood by the reader. Sight words are learned as complete units, as whole words. It is important for a reader to develop a large and growing command of such words in order to reach the major goal of reading—to understand the meaning of what is being read. Learning to recognize and identify words by sight is an essential part of any reading program. Be careful not to use lists of words that have little meaning to the students. Experience texts or writings, whether dictated or written by the students, and printed material in the students' interest areas, can provide a rich source of sight words.

Sight words are taught by having the learners look at one word at a time and associating the printed word with the spoken word. Your students know the meanings of most of the words because they come from their own vocabularies and from their own stories and printed materials in their interest areas.

Building a sight word (or memorized) vocabulary is a part of tutoring at all reading levels. When students recognize many words in a sentence on sight, they can often figure out the meaning of the entire sentence and thus read words in their spoken vocabulary that they would not otherwise be able to read. This ability to note what makes sense in a passage is called using context clues. The use of context clues is a skill that all good readers possess.

For example, in the sentence "I want to l_____ more about the world," new readers might predict accurately that the word beginning with l is *learn* if they know the other words in the sentence and the sound of *l*, and if *learn* is in their speaking vocabularies.

A sight vocabulary helps readers predict what words are most likely to make sense in a given story, increases reading fluency, and leads to better comprehension.

TYPES OF SIGHT WORDS

There are four types of words you will want to teach as sight words:

1. Survival words.

2. Service or utility words.

3. Irregularly spelled words.

4. Introductory words in word patterns (rhyming words).

Survival words are those words that students need immediately in day-to-day living. These can be related to safety, jobs, consumerism, family—whatever students need to be able to read. Safety-related survival words include *danger, police, hospital, emergency,* and *poison.* Examples of job-related survival words are *social security, company, office worker, official,* and *deduction.* Consumer-related survival words include *post office, sale, repair, bank, loan,* and *warranty.*

Service or utility words like *the, a, and, but, when, where, how,* and *why* occur frequently in written material but are often not phonetically regular. They are abstract and do not bring to mind any mental images to aid understanding.

Irregularly spelled words such as *of, have, who,* and *give* must also be taught as sight words.

Introductory words in a patterned series (see pages 66-71) are usually taught as sight words. Thus, *make* would be taught as a sight word if it is not already known from the *-ake* pattern. *Bake* and *cake* would then be taught as patterned words.

SELECTING SIGHT WORDS

Sight words will occur naturally in your students' language experience stories and other materials such as books, manuals, newspapers, notices, signs, forms, and survival word lists.

A WORD ABOUT WORD LISTS

Sometimes tutors find themselves in the trap of teaching lists instead of teaching reading. The key is to use lists that are relevant to individual learners. A homemaker usually keeps a list of items needed at the store. A security officer might need a checklist while making the rounds. Many of us keep lists of things we must do: make a dental appointment, call the school, check on the telephone bill. These lists can be used as teaching tools.

Memorizing lists of unrelated words—that is, words unrelated to the topic of the lesson, to each other, or to the learners' needs—is of little value. A worthwhile activity might be for you and your students to construct personal word lists.

TEACHING SIGHT WORDS

Select, with your students, a limited number of words from the material you are reading to be taught as sight words. Six to eight new sight words per lesson are generally appropriate. You may find it necessary to select fewer for some students in the beginning as you build confidence. After working with your students for a while, you will be better able to judge how many words they can handle.

Ask your students to pick one word. Ask them to write the new sight word in manuscript on a small card. (If a student is a nonwriting beginner, you, the tutor, can write the word on a card.) Students who can write in cursive may want to write the word in cursive on the other side of the card.

Have the students put the word into a new sentence. Either you or your students can write the new sentence on a piece of paper. Also, you might want to put this sentence on the reverse side of the card. Putting the word into a context clarifies its meaning and provides clues for remembering the word.

Have your students read the word while looking at the word card and then match the word card to its mate in the sentence, saying the word as it is being matched.

Go on to the next word if the match is completed. Repeat the above until you have introduced all the sight words for that lesson. If the match is not completed, review the word and new sentence. Avoid excessive repetition as it only frustrates the students.

Ask the students to shuffle the word cards and practice rereading them, returning to the written sentences as necessary. File "known" word cards, and keep separate those that need more practice.

A general rule is that students "know" any word they can read out of context at three separate sessions. It is helpful to put a check on the back of the word card if they can read it correctly and then use it in a sentence. Three checks on a word card indicates the word is "known." As soon as your students can read a word easily over more than three lessons, that word can be put into a file box as a known word.

SIMILAR LOOKING WORDS

At some time your students may confuse words that look alike (*went, want*). In this case, it is helpful to teach one of them so thoroughly that the sight of it calls forth an immediate response. For example, have the students do the following:

1. Read the word aloud from the word card.

2. Place the word in a sentence.

3. Write the word as it is said.

4. Name the letters that compose the word.

Remove the other word that originally caused confusion and do not introduce this word until the first word has been so thoroughly learned that confusion is no longer likely. This is called *over-learning*. The second word of the pair may be introduced later without difficulty because the earlier learning is so complete that your students no longer need to consciously think about what the word is.

One of the skills that you want your students to have is the ability to recognize the same words in many contexts. But remember, beginning readers have to see a new word many times before it becomes part of their sight vocabulary. You will need to provide much practice within varied contexts to help word recognition become automatic.

CHECKLIST

Sight Words

1. You and your students select words to be taught as sight words from experience stories, reading material, students' personal lists, or students' survival word lists.

2. Ask your students to pick one word.

3. Write or have the students write the word in manuscript on a small card (in cursive, too, on the reverse side, if a student writes in cursive).

4. Ask the students to put the word in a new sentence. You or the students can write the new sentence on a piece of paper and on the back of the word card.

5. Teach the word by having the students read the word aloud while looking at the word card.

6. Have your students match the word card to the word in the sentence, saying the word as it is being matched.

7. Go on to the next word if the sequence is completed. If not, go back to Step 5.

8. Ask the students to shuffle the word cards and practice rereading them.

9. File known word cards. Keep others for additional practice.

CONTEXT CLUES

You will want to give your students a great deal of practice in using context to predict words. This will keep your students focused on reading for meaning from the very first lessons. With very beginning readers you could use traffic signs like STOP, other signs like WOMEN or MEN, or items such as checks, menus, and forms to introduce the targeted sight word. The context is then the form or sign itself.

THE CLOZE PROCEDURE

One way to gain proficiency in the use of context clues is to use a variation of the cloze procedure for practice. In this procedure, a person supplies words which have been deleted from a text. This technique demonstrates that people use their knowledge of the world and of language to predict as they read, that reading is a combination of many factors all operating at once. Encourage your students to predict or guess as they read. Do not interrupt them to correct substitutions. Give time for self-correction. If that does not occur, note what kind of substitution was made and check at the end of the reading. If a word with the same meaning has been substituted, just point to the word missed and ask if the learners can read it. If a word with a completely different meaning has been substituted, ask comprehension questions about the meaning of the sentence. Supply the correct word if you sense frustration. To prepare materials for cloze exercises, any of the following techniques may be used:

1. Use materials easily read by the students. Delete words that require students to use either parts of speech or meaning clues to replace the word logically. Supply one logical replacement and another choice. Have the students read through the activity, searching for the words that make sense:

   Just as _____ have fur, birds have _____.
        (coats, animals)   (feathers, wings)

   I go to the farmer's market to buy fresh _____ and _____.
                                               (pencils, vegetables)   (plants, books)

2. When learners have used the technique described above and can replace the appropriate words from the choices supplied, provide passages in which every fifth word or every tenth word is arbitrarily deleted and only a letter or two of the correct word is available, perhaps a beginning consonant or consonant blend:

   With the price of f_____ going up all the t_____, more people are trying
   t_____ raise some of their f_____ in their own back y_____.

*With the price of food going up all the time, more people are trying
to raise some of their food in their own back yard.*

57

3. When the learners do well with this task, indicate only the blank with no additional clues. Accept any word that seems a reasonable fit:

Instead of grass, you _____ rows of lettuce, tomatoes, _____ beans lining the fences _____ in the biggest city.

Instead of grass, you find rows of lettuce, tomatoes, and beans lining the fences even in the biggest city.

There are many computer programs that teach sight words through cloze activities.

PHONICS: LETTER-SOUND RELATIONSHIPS

Phonics is the one technique which takes longer to demonstrate in a text than to teach. Most adults know the names of the letters, but phonics helps students discover the connections between *letters* and *sounds*. Many students may already know these connections. Through your early assessment, if you find your students know all the letter-sound correspondences, then there is no need for phonics instruction. However, if you find a student has trouble with a few or all specific letter-sound combinations, you can use this technique.

As a base for understanding phonics instruction, it is useful to know that we use thousands of words in talking, reading, and writing, but only 26 letters are used to spell these words. These 26 letters are called the *alphabet*. They represent 42-44 sounds. Most of the letters in the alphabet are called *consonants*. Five of the letters—*a, e, i, o, u*—are called *vowels*. Sometimes *y* is used as a vowel.

Point to a letter in a word and explain to your students that each letter is a symbol. Explain that words are made up of groups of letters. Point to an entire sentence and explain that a sentence is made up of a group of words. Note that the first word of a sentence begins with a capital letter and that most sentences end with a period.

Because people learn in different ways that are not always predictable or completely understood, successful reading and writing instruction can often be accomplished best by using several approaches at the same time. Some people seem to learn words as a whole. Many words in English should be learned this way because they do not break down readily into sound units. Other words can be recognized through the analysis of letters and letter clusters.

There are many ways to teach letter-sound relationships. Any way is acceptable if it works with your students. The important thing is that your students associate sounds with letters and groups of letters. After learning a basic technique, you may find other creative ideas to teach letter-sound relationships. Adapt the system to meet each student's needs.

Many students are not aware of the complexity of sounds that make up a spoken word. Students will vary in their ability to perceive sounds. This may be evidence of a hearing problem. Since many of these problems are correctable and will affect learning to read, students may find it useful to get hearing tests if at all possible.

Remember, too, that some people can hear very well but cannot distinguish one sound from another in speech and/or hearing. They may lack auditory discrimination of one sound or perhaps several sounds. If that is the situation, they may have a good deal of trouble with phonics instruction. You will probably need to tread lightly, being careful not to frustrate students. Use other strategies.

To decide if auditory discrimination may be the problem, take two words that sound exactly alike except for one sound (for example, *set* and *sit* or *mat* and *met* or *pot* and *put;* for native speakers of the English language, vowels are usually the tricky ones). If you find that your students cannot distinguish your pronunciation of *sit* from *set,* you may have students with auditory discrimination problems. You will only frustrate them if you try to get them to read or write based on a sound distinction that they may never have heard or said.

Remember, too, that speakers of different dialect communities vary pronunciation and do not themselves differentiate in the pronunciation of certain sounds. For example, some communities say *witch* and *which* the same way. Others pronounce *pen* and *pin* the same. Still others equate *Yale* and *yell.* Being aware of differences in pronunciation and complications from problems with auditory discrimination can help you be sensitive to students who do not respond well to phonics instruction. Above all, if students pronounce a word differently from the way you do, do not tell them they are wrong; they are not. Their sound system is just different from yours.

Begin by teaching the letters that each individual student needs—those identified in the student's assessment.

However, you cannot teach your students to use these letter-sound relationships unless you know them yourself. If you are unsure of the sounds, review them aloud, listening carefully as you pronounce the words related to each letter as suggested in the Appendix on page 169.

If students are complete nonreaders, you may want to teach only one letter per lesson. Remember, you'll be introducing experience stories and sight words, too. If phonics work is needed, be sure to keep the phonics part of each lesson short and related to the material being used. Phonic exercises may be tiring to your students. Tell your students why phonics is an important part of the lesson, that to recognize the sounds that letters represent will help identify new words.

Only paper and a pen or pencil—no specific books—are needed for teaching phonics. You will want to look at the list of Suggested Key Words on page 169. You can supplement this list with words from your students' experience writings as well as from newspapers, magazines, and available books—words to which the students can relate.

These exercises are meant for those who need help in learning all letter names and sounds. Don't re-teach phonic skills if your students already recognize letters and their corresponding sounds. But if you find students who consistently miscall the sound of a specific letter, perhaps mixing *d* and *b*, or not knowing the sound for *k* or *w*, use this technique to assist them. If you find that letter-sound instruction frustrates or confuses students, emphasize some other techniques. Before attempting to teach, carefully study the instructions provided. In the teaching examples that follow, letter names are shown as *s, f*; letter sounds are shown as /*s*/, /*f*/.

CONSONANTS

You and your students will be creating a letter-sound dictionary as you proceed with the instructions that follow. Provide one sheet of paper or a 3" x 5" card for each letter, using the following format for teaching consonants.

Action	*Tutor Says*	*Student's Response*
Tutor writes *s* in manuscript and points to it. *s*	This is an *s*.	
	What is the name of this letter?	*s*
	Listen for the sound of *s* at the beginning of these words—*sun, sink, socks, sandwich.* Do you hear the sound?	yes
	Say these words after me while listening for the beginning sound: *sun* *sink* *socks* *sandwich*	*sun* *sink* *socks* *sandwich*

Action	Tutor Says	Student's Response
	Which of these *s* words— *sun, sink, socks, sandwich*— do you want for your key word to help you remember the sound of *s*?	(Student selects word. Let's assume the word *sun* is selected.)

(A key word will always mean more if the student can identify with it. Words beginning with blends such as *snake* or *tree* should not be used as key words. It is easier for the student to use a word with a single consonant beginning. You might suggest a key word from an experience story. You should make sure that key words are words students can "see." For example, *best* is not a good key word because it does not evoke a mental picture. Better key words would be *bus, baby,* or *bed* because students can visualize these objects.)

Action	Tutor Says	Student's Response
Tutor writes student's key word in manuscript under *s*.	*Sun* is your key word to help you remember the sound of *s*.	

```
s
sun
```

Action	Tutor Says	Student's Response
	Think of the beginning sound in *sun*. Now, let out just the first sound. In the beginning you may need to say, "Notice how you hold your lips, tongue, and teeth."	/s/

(If the student, within a reasonable time, fails to make the desired response, you might supply it: /s/ is the sound of the letter *s*.)

Action	Tutor Says	Student's Response
	Here are some words. Listen. Do these words start with the *s* sound?	
	sausage	yes
	forest	no
	Monday	no
	salad	yes
	summer	yes

61

Action	Tutor Says	Student's Response
	Now, let's move this sound to the end of the word. Listen to the last sound in these words, and repeat the words:	
	gas	*gas*
	kiss	*kiss*
	boss	*boss*
	What is the last sound in these words?	/s/
Tutor points to *s*.	What is the name of this letter?	*s*

> *s*
> *sun*

Action	Tutor Says	Student's Response
Tutor points to *sun*.	What is your key word?	*sun*
	What is the sound of *s*?	/s/
Student writes as tutor points.	Will you write an *s* right here?	

> *s*   *s*
> *sun*

(A beginning student may need more writing practice of individual letters, using your manuscript letters as models.)

Action	*Tutor Says*	*Student's Response*
Tutor prints capital *S*.	This is a capital *S*, the same name, the same sound. You use a capital letter for a name that begins with *S* or the first word in a sentence.	

s S   *s S*
sun

(If your student already writes in cursive, you and the student should write the *s* and *S* in cursive, too.)

(More written words can be added to the *s* page later.)

s S   *s S*
sun
sink
sandwich

If your students learn quickly and if phonics is a review, it is not necessary to have a separate page for each letter. You might want to put all the letters and individual words on one sheet for home study.

You may prefer to use 3" x 5" cards instead of sheets of paper. Use one card for each letter, having the students write the letter and the key word on them. This is convenient for review.

Use the preceding format to practice the instructional procedures for the consonants. You should be thoroughly familiar with the instructional procedure before you begin teaching your students.

This practice may seem excessive, but experience has shown that thorough familiarity with these procedures is essential to your success with this technique.

LETTER-SOUND ACTIVITIES

Some students have problems distinguishing individual sounds in words. If, after reasonable instruction, you fail to note any progress in relating sounds to letters, instruct by reading to your students, having them follow along using the sight word technique. You might want to try again a little later on to see if they can learn letter-sound associations.

When working on letters and sounds with students who can read only a very limited number of words, give them something to do that looks like reading. Using a newspaper, have the students look for the known letters (perhaps circling them) and review the names of the letters, key words, and sounds. This is an effective way of using the newspaper at the level of even a beginning student's ability.

Your students could also spell the beginning and ending letters of a word. Point to objects around the room, such as the door, a book, some paper, a pen, and ask your students to name the objects and then identify the beginning and ending sounds. Use only items that incorporate known sounds.

Phonics (Consonants)

1. Tutor names the letter. Tutor writes it. Student repeats the letter name.

2. Student listens for the sound of the letter at the beginning of some words while the tutor says the words and then while the student says them.

3. Student picks a key word. Tutor writes the word.

4. Student produces the sound of the letter by producing the beginning sound of the key word.

5. Student listens and recognizes the sound in the beginning of other words.

6. Student listens and recognizes the sound at the end of words.

7. Student produces the sound at the end of words.

8. Student and tutor review the name, sound, and key word for the letter.

9. Student writes the letter.

10. Tutor explains and writes the capital letter.

CONSONANT BLENDS

If your student has learned words that begin or end with single consonants, it is now possible to teach blends without requiring any new knowledge. Blends are two consonants in a row with the two sounds blending together (*bl*, *cr*). Merely blend in the additional consonant with the word the student already knows. For example, if the learner knows *lag* as a word, the addition of the consonant *f* (representing the sound /*f*/) will yield *flag*. *Top* becomes *stop* by the simple addition of one letter sound. *Ben* becomes *bent* or *bend* when the sound of either *t* or *d* is added at the end. The most frequently occurring blends have *r* or *l* in the second position (*tr*, *cl*).

CONSONANT DIGRAPHS

When teaching the digraphs (two letters with only one sound, *sh*, *ch*, *th*, *wh*, and *qu*), follow the same format used in teaching single consonants. Note that the sound for *th* in words like *thumb* is slightly different than in words like *the*. The *th* in *thumb* is voiceless and the *th* in *the* is voiced. It is not important to stress this distinction.

VOWELS

Vowels are a major challenge in learning to read because they represent so many sounds. Frequently the sound the vowel represents can only be determined by noting the letters that follow it. Note the many ways *a* can sound in various patterns.

> *man*
>
> *mar*
>
> *mean*
>
> *make*
>
> *maw*

It is interesting to see how difficult it is to supply the correct consonant sound to complete the pattern when all you have are vowels. For example try to read this sentence:

E_e_ _i_ _ a_ _ _ _e _o_e_ _ _e_ _ ou_ , _ou _i_ _ _o_i_e _ _a_
_ou _a_ _ea_ _ _i_ _e_ _e_ _e _ui_e ea_i_ _.

By contrast, try to read this sentence:

_v_n w_th _ll th_ v_w_ls l_ft _ _t, y_ _ w_ll n_t_c_ th_t y_ _ c_n
r_ _d th_s s_nt_nc_ q_ _t_ _ _s_ly.

Yes, when you have the consonants, the passage is very easy to read.

Even with all the vowels left out, you will notice that you can read this sentence quite easily.

Most students know letter names. For the occasional students who don't know the names of the vowels, teach them the names and how to write them in both manuscript and cursive.

A WORD ABOUT PHONIC RULES

English is not a phonetically regular language. Many of the rules formerly incorporated into phonics programs have so many exceptions that they may be more confusing than enlightening to students. For example, the rule that two vowels together usually represent the long sound of the first vowel (words such as *meat, die, dough)* is accurate for words in beginning reading books only 45% of the time. For words from a dictionary, this rule applies only 18% of the time. Consider words such as *great, threat, relieve, heard,* and *sieve.*

65

Many reading systems teach rules for dividing words into syllables with appropriate accenting. The usefulness of such rules is questionable, since the application of the rule often requires that students already be able to pronounce the word. For example, while it is asserted that each syllable in a word has one vowel sound, it is not true that this vowel is always heard. Consider the final syllable in words like *sudden, leader,* and *system,* and compare the sounds of these syllables with the consonant sounds you have just learned. The vowel sound is suppressed and the consonant predominates in normal speech patterns.

It is also untrue that each vowel in a word provides its own vowel sound (*rain, made*). Therefore, if students look at a word in an effort to be able to pronounce it, they may have great difficulty in deciding which cluster of letters constitutes a syllable. This process can become so complicated that students who could follow such directions would certainly be capable of learning the word anyway.

WORD PATTERNS

Learning words by seeing word patterns enables the students to notice more readily the relationships between clusters of letters and the sounds they represent. The most prevalent letter cluster in English is the consonant-vowel-consonant (C-V-C). Here are samples of two word families of patterns:

get	*cap*
set	*map*
let	*sap*
met	*tap*

Parts of words that sound alike are often spelled alike.

RHYMING

Before you begin instruction in word patterns, it is helpful to know if your students understand rhyming. Some adult nonreaders have not been exposed to nursery rhymes as children and may not understand that *cat* and *rat* rhyme. Such students may not even know what the word *rhyme* means. When a word rhymes with another, it agrees with that word in the ending sounds.

If your students cannot rhyme words, this technique might help. Provide your students with several rhyming words of more than one syllable, then a beginning sound to which the rhyming ending will be attached. For example, say:

"I am going to give you three rhyming words. Then I'll start the fourth word and you finish it like the rest. Listen:

colder

bolder

holder

/f/

The students should reply *"folder."* If not, supply the word and repeat the series. Then give another example, such as:

> *jacket*
> *packet*
> */r/*

Supply again, if necessary, *"racket."* Continue to give such models until the students understand rhyming. The reason for using larger words is that the students are given a greater number of common elements to help in understanding the notion of rhyming.

Once you are sure of the students' ability to rhyme, you can move to shorter clusters:

> *ran*
> *man*
> *can*
> */f/*

with assurance that students hear the common sound and also see the letters that represent these identical clusters of sounds. Often this is a simple task, but for some students it's a challenge.

TEACHING WORD PATTERNS

Choose a patterned word from the words your students already know. Use a simple consonant-vowel-consonant (C-V-C) word first. You will take this known word and analyze it into its beginning letter and the C-V-C pattern you want to teach. Remind your students what the word is. This first word is the clue from which they will figure out the rest of the words in that pattern. Always list the words vertically so that the common visual characteristics are noticed by the students.

Vowels are taught as part of ending clusters because the sound that a vowel represents is usually signaled by the pattern in which it is found. Therefore, if your students learn a sound cluster—such as *-an*—as a unit, it will be more helpful than to sound out words by pronouncing each sound individually.

The basic approach to teaching word patterns involves blending the consonants with a letter grouping called a phonogram (*-at*, *-eg*, *-ick*, *-end*). About 100 of these phonograms combined with consonants will provide students with many words—enough to indicate the general meaning of a passage. The context clues in addition to consonants will allow the students to infer most other words. These word patterns or phonograms may be taught in the following way:

WORD PATTERNS

Action	Tutor Says	Students' Response
Tutor writes *cap*. *cap*	This word is *cap*. What is this word?	*cap*
Tutor writes *map* directly under *cap*. *cap* *map*	If *c-a-p* is *cap*, what is *m-a-p*? (If there is no answer or an incorrect answer, supply *map*.)	*map*
Tutor writes *lap*. *cap* *map* *lap*	And what is *l-a-p*?	*lap*
Tutor writes *sap*. *cap* *map* *lap* *sap*	And what is *s-a-p*?	*sap*
	Please reread the whole list.	*cap* *map* *lap* *sap*
	What is the same in each word?	The *-ap*.

(Accept the sounds of the pattern or the letters.)

If your students are struggling to understand this new concept, use only three or four words in a pattern. Too many words may be confusing. More words can be added later.

For more advanced students, use more difficult words from experience stories, workbooks, or any other reading material being used. For the students who understand this concept, the possibilities are unlimited. Many words can be learned, such as:

sing	*sight*
ring	*right*
bring	*might*
spring	*bright*
string	*blight*

The technique of teaching patterned words may seem deceptively simple. Students may need to expend considerable effort until they see that words having common letter clusters often have common sound clusters. It is worthwhile to continue to use this technique even when it does not bring immediate success. Its power is immense when students catch on.

There are, however, some students who do not seem to be able to learn an entire letter grouping as one unit. For these students, sounding out separate letters may be a necessary first step. This individual letter-sounding should be abandoned as soon as possible.

If, for example, your student, in reading the word *got*, says *get:*

1. Ask the student to name the letters.

2. If this does not produce *got,* say, "You gave me *g-e-t.* The word is spelled *g-o-t.*" Emphasize the letter in question.

3. If this does not produce the correct pronunciation, write *not* and ask the student to read it. Then write *got* below it, soliciting a response.

4. If the word is still not pronounced, supply it.

5. Add patterned words in a column to help produce the generalization of the pattern, such as:

> *not*
> *got*
> *hot*
> *pot*
> *dot*
> *cot*

As your students progress, the initial consonant substitution is not always necessary because you want instant recognition of larger letter clusters. The goal is to have your students recognize the entire letter cluster, such as *man* in *manage* or *sat* in *satisfy*. Such clusters provide the structure for words with more than one syllable. Learning many such clusters establishes the basis for independent word attack.

This method emphasizes the vowel as part of the word pattern rather than in isolation. Most students will find this less confusing than to remember distinctions between long vowels, short vowels, vowels affected by *r, l, w*, etc.

There are lists of patterned words in the Appendix on pages 170-180.

LONG VOWEL SOUNDS IN PATTERN

It is easy to identify a long vowel sound in spoken words because the sound is the same as the letter name. It is often more difficult to identify the long vowel sounds in written words because in English the sound is represented by so many different letter clusters. For example, the long vowel *o* might be spelled as follows:

> *o* as in *so*
> *oa* as in *coat*
> *oe* as in *toe*
> *ow* as in *blow*
> *ough* as in *dough*
> *eau* as in *beau*

Teach clusters of words giving the long vowel sound by using the word pattern procedure on page 68. You would teach:

> *coat*
> *boat*
> *goat*

in one long *o* pattern and

> *toe*
> *foe*
> *hoe*

at another session.

In addition, clusters that look alike often result in different sounds. For example:

> *ew* as in *sew* is different from *ew* in *blew*
> *ow* in *now* is different from *ow* in *show*
> *ou* as in *found* is different from *ou* in *group, young, four, though* or *thought*

It is usually easier to teach one of the sound patterns (*cow, now, how*) before teaching the other pattern (*low, slow, blow*).

In reading a passage, if your students come across unknown words with spellings that can have more than one sound, suggest that they try both sounds and select the word that makes sense in that sentence.

Once your students understand the concept of rhyming, word patterns are easy to teach and fun to work with. Enjoy this technique and use it often.

CHECKLIST

Word Patterns

1. Tutor writes the first word in a pattern, saying the letters and the word.

2. Tutor writes the second pattern word directly under the first, using a beginning sound the students know. Tutor asks the students to read the word.

3. If the students respond correctly, the tutor adds more words in pattern asking the students to read the words.

   If the students give no response or a wrong response, the tutor reviews possible elements of difficulty:

   a. The students may not remember the beginning sound.

   b. The students may not remember the sound of the letter cluster.

4. Tutor asks the students to read the list of patterned words.

5. Tutor asks the students to identify the letters that are the same in all the words. Tutor accepts the sounds of the pattern or the names of the letters.

6. Tutor and students make word cards for the words in each pattern.

ANALYZING MULTI-SYLLABIC WORDS INTO PATTERNS

As your students are learning to recognize patterns, looking for patterns in words of more than one syllable within the reading materials can be helpful. By pronouncing identified patterns within longer words, students will be able to handle these words more easily. They can check their pronunciation of the word against their knowledge of what word would make sense in that context. For example, the word *passenger* is composed of three already familiar patterns:

   pas / sen / ger

   If the students should happen to look at the word in a slightly different way, dividing it as

   pass / en / ger

will still result in a similar pronunciation.

These word divisions may not be the traditional syllables you find in a dictionary, but it is not necessary to divide words precisely as the dictionary does in order to use this skill in multi-syllabic words. Indeed, dictionaries do not always agree on how a given word should be broken down. It is essential for your students to be able to handle the groups of letters that comprise the word.

Using the following steps try out this skill on words such as *transportation, merchandise, combination.*

1. Students look at the word to determine what familiar patterns it contains.

2. Students indicate the clusters by marking the word with a pencil:

   trans / por / ta / tion

3. Tutor asks the students to pronounce each letter cluster as quickly as possible, blending them into the word. Any pronounceable combination is acceptable. If there is a slight mispronunciation, the students should recognize the word if it is known in oral language.

4. Tutor encourages the students to use the meaning clues in order to get a correct pronunciation.

5. If the students cannot do this easily, the tutor divides one or two words as examples.

   buf / fa / lo

   en / vel / ope

The important thing is to have your students look for recognizable letter clusters. Start with whatever part of the word your students know. Suggest that they first look for a part of the word that is familiar. Often they recognize the first syllable; sometimes they recognize the one in the middle, as in the word *struggle.* They may recognize

   rug

then

   trug
   strug / gle

Not all words divide easily to produce a near approximation in sound to the word in question. It is just as logical to divide *apron* as *ap / ron* or *a / pron, business* as *bus / in / ess* or *bus / i / ness,* or *razor* as *raz / or* or *ra / zor,* but a search for meaning usually brings forth the desired recognition of the word.

Application of the skills you have taught and the clues that come from the context itself should allow the students to pronounce the word correctly. It is helpful to start with compound words that are easy to divide (ones that consist of two complete words such as *hallway, upstairs)*, or with words having prefixes or suffixes (such as *compound, reflex* or *action, teller).*

CHECKLIST

Multi-Syllabic Words

1. Students look at the word, searching for familiar patterns *(outstanding).*

2. Students indicate letter clusters by slash marks *(out / stand / ing).*

3. Students pronounce each letter cluster, quickly blending into a word.

4. Students check against the context clues, asking "Does this make sense here?"

VAKT APPROACH

If learning is difficult for your students, you may want to use some or all of the techniques described in the Visual-Auditory-Kinesthetic-Tactile (VAKT) approach. This approach has been around for years and has been helpful in many cases.

VISUAL

Take a word card and hold it in front of your students saying, "Look at the word, picturing it exactly the way you'd take a picture of a friend. Say the word." (Students respond.) "Now close your eyes and picture the word in your mind. Can you see the word?" (Students respond.) "Now, open your eyes and look at the card again. What is the word?" (Students respond.)

This technique may not work in all cases, since there are some people who do not get mental images well. This capability does not necessarily depend on a person's intellectual level. If your students say they cannot see the picture, you might suggest they close their eyes again and picture a child's face or a best friend's face. If this results in a picture, repetition of the above technique will be beneficial. If the students are not capable of getting mental pictures, abandon the closing of the eyes technique and simply teach by looking at the card directly.

AUDITORY

Auditory techniques take into account the sound elements of a word and may provide a clue to at least part of a word. This gives the learners a place to begin in word identification. Say the word slowly as it appears on the word card or in the material being read. Read it in a phrase or sentence to the learners, asking them to follow along as you read. Ask them to repeat what you have said. Sometimes the sound of the learners' own voices helps memorization. It may take many repetitions before the learners recognize the word. In this way, you are modeling the letter-sound relationship as the word or the pattern is being memorized.

If there is difficulty, draw the learners' attention to the beginning, middle, or ending consonant—this may serve as a cue. The goal, however, is to recognize the word, not to pronounce each letter in turn.

KINESTHETIC

For words of two, three, or four letters, it is often helpful, if the letters are known, to ask your students to use their index fingers to write the word in the air, on the table, or on paper. The letters of that word are thus fixed in the mind, and another sensory pathway for recall of the word is provided.

If this is difficult, write the word large enough for your students to trace over with their fingers (not a pencil or pen). When they have traced it several times, remove the copy and have them write the word from memory, saying each part of the word as it is written. If your students make an error, cover the writing and go back to the tracing step. Have them continue this process until the word can be easily and correctly written.

TACTILE

Some students can be helped by forming letters in a pan of damp sand or sugar using the index finger. The feel of rough sand and the pressure needed to form the letters help some students remember the letter forms and the words. You might also use sandpaper or different types of textured materials to help your students feel a letter. This is often an effective way to help a person sense the difference between *b* and *d*.

A way to provide a raised impression of the word for your students is to write it in large letters with a wax crayon on a sheet of paper placed on a piece of window screening. This will provide an embossed impression of the word which can then be felt by your students as they trace the word with their fingers.

SUMMARY

Most beginning students are blocked in reading and writing fluency by their inability to recognize printed words quickly and accurately. You now have a number of approaches to help your students learn to do this.

Throughout your teaching, check that your students understand what they're reading and writing. Without comprehension, true reading has not taken place.

All of this will probably take much time. There will be high peaks of sudden discovery and long plateaus where progress may not be so dramatic. As you teach, go back to your notes on students and to early assessments. You'll probably find more progress than you would have believed possible.

♦♦♦

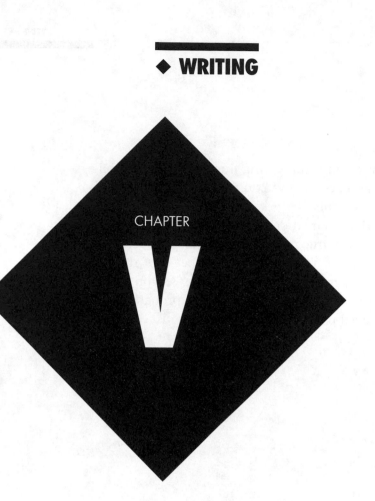

◆ **WRITING**

CHAPTER

V

WRITING

ONE OF THE THEMES OF THIS BOOK is that we view language as a whole, consisting of listening, speaking, reading, and writing, as mediated through thinking. Furthermore, successful teaching programs recognize that the best teaching occurs when these language components are not taught in isolation from each other. Though this chapter is about writing, a great deal of emphasis is given to reading, speaking, and listening as they relate to the writing process.

In this chapter you will find a general discussion of the process writing cycle as well as specific examples using this cycle in two lessons for goal setting: one in a one-to-one situation with a beginning level student and the other with a small group.

Writing is one approach to problem solving. It doesn't just happen in a tutoring session; it happens every day—in the family, at work, in religious groups, and in social settings. A collaborative writing process can be used whether you teach in a one-to-one situation or in a small group. Because the writing process constantly requires reading of material being generated, it helps reinforce reading ability. It is never too soon to begin writing activities—even with new writers.

THE WRITING PROCESS

Whoever said there's nothing new under the sun was right; or, at least, there's nothing new about process writing except its name. We have all gone through the process at one time or another.

Think of a time you bought something, an expensive watch, for example, and it didn't work. What did you do?

Chances are, you fussed and fumed at whoever would listen. You and another person or small group of people talked about the options you had. You might have decided to write a letter of complaint or call the Better Business Bureau. If you called, you probably practiced what you were going to say before you made your call. If you wrote, you probably drafted a letter, read it to and discussed it with someone else, fixed it, rewrote it, read it, until you and your audience were satisfied, and then you sent that letter on its way.

When we have problems, we often solve them through discussion, writing, reading, more discussion, and rewriting. Have you ever solved a problem in this manner? If so, you have used the same steps that make up process writing.

Process writing, which emphasizes discussion, reading, and writing in collaboration with another person or a small group, is often just a way to solve a problem.

The writing process can be broken down into broad parts for the purpose of discussion. (Process writing, the writing process, and the writing cycle are three terms that are used interchangeably throughout this chapter as well as in professional and scholarly journals.)

This process should not be viewed as a lock-step procedure. It may be helpful to think of the steps in the writing process as floors of a building. You can take the elevator from the basement to the third floor and up to the fourth. In other words, you can move up or down, can revisit floors, can go back to the bottom and start over.

In fact, many professional writers frequently move back and forth between steps as they add and delete details, reorder the sequence of information, edit for mechanics, or put a piece away to be dealt with at another time.

The following illustrates how the steps fit into the lesson structure.

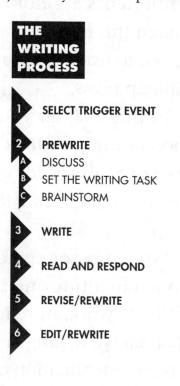

THE WRITING PROCESS

1 **SELECT TRIGGER EVENT**

2 **PREWRITE**
  A DISCUSS
  B SET THE WRITING TASK
  C BRAINSTORM

3 **WRITE**

4 **READ AND RESPOND**

5 **REVISE/REWRITE**

6 **EDIT/REWRITE**

STEP 1. SELECT TRIGGER EVENT

The trigger event is what starts the discussion. It can be in print (e.g., a story that you read to the students or the students read together) but it doesn't have to be. In fact, it can be just about any-thing—a picture, a movie, a piece of art work, the local news, a topic of general concern, a problem, or a meaningful experience. Trigger events are usu-ally more successful in prompting discussion if they are of interest to the student or the group and if they are phrased as a specific question.

For example, "What did you do last sum-mer?" is usually not an effective trigger event for two reasons: 1. Few people care what we did last summer. 2. Most people's answer would be "Noth-ing much." A better trigger event could be, "What has been the most exciting day of your life?" or "What has been the most unusual thing you've ever done?" The students then will have a specific question to respond to, a question that evokes a positive, emotional response.

In the first meeting, the tutor may want to set the trigger event. Later, this could be the responsibility of the student or the small group. For a small group formed for a par-ticular purpose (e.g., getting a driver's license, reading to children), the focus of the group will help determine the trigger event.

THE WRITING PROCESS

1 ▶ SELECT TRIGGER EVENT

2 ▶ PREWRITE
A DISCUSS
B SET THE WRITING TASK
C BRAINSTORM

3 ▶ WRITE

4 ▶ READ AND RESPOND

5 ▶ REVISE/REWRITE

6 ▶ EDIT/REWRITE

STEP 2. PREWRITE

Prewriting activities include all those activities that come before the writer begins to draft a piece of writ-ing. These include a good deal of discussion, brain-storming about topics, thinking about logical ways of presenting ideas, making notes or outlines, and narrowing of topics into specific and manageable tasks. In this stage writers need to determine their purpose and audience. They need to clarify why they are writing and to whom.

STEP 2A. DISCUSS

The tutor asks questions regarding the trigger event to start a conversation and let ideas flow.

THE WRITING PROCESS

1 ▶ SELECT TRIGGER EVENT

2 ▶ PREWRITE
A DISCUSS
B SET THE WRITING TASK
C BRAINSTORM

3 ▶ WRITE

4 ▶ READ AND RESPOND

5 ▶ REVISE/REWRITE

6 ▶ EDIT/REWRITE

79

In this situation, the trigger event often points to student goals. The tutor asks questions about the trigger event to prompt discussion. Ask, don't tell. If you use a movie or video, the trigger question to start a discussion could be, "Well, what do you think?" or "What characters made the biggest impression on you and why?" You are looking for questions that will produce responses of more than one or two words (open-ended responses). Once you elicit the responses, then ask, "Why?" or "Could you tell me more about that?"

STEP 2B. SET THE WRITING TASK

Move from discussion to a specific writing task: "Shall we write a letter, book/movie review, a story, a poem?" Or perhaps the writing task could be a report for work.

STEP 2C. BRAINSTORM

Brainstorming is the open-ended process of getting ideas out and bandying them about. Begin with a broad question focused on the writing task: "What might we say about . . . ?"

As you brainstorm together to answer that question, it is helpful to jot down key words, words that will remind the students of specific things they have talked about. This list of key words can serve as a first outline of the writing.

To expand and explain the key words and how they connect, a mapping (or clustering) strategy can be used. This can be done at the brainstorming stage as well as later at a rewriting stage. Mapping helps students put additional ideas on their writing subjects into words, seeing how and where they can expand their key words and ideas. From the key words, have the students say what comes to mind as they reread each word, jotting down the new words as an extension of each key word. For example, suppose parents want to write a letter about their concern for the local schools. Their key phrases might be: *support school*, *children suffer*, and *education to get jobs*. Mapping could look like this diagram.

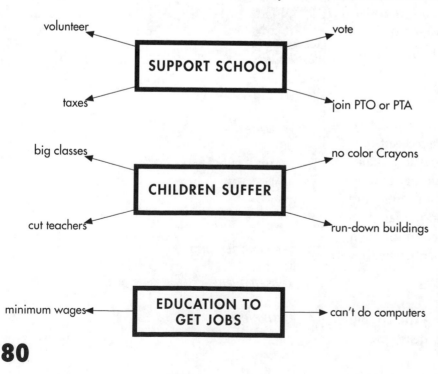

As a tutor, a facilitator of discussion, you can write the trigger event, the task, and the key words as a rough outline on the board, a flip chart, or even a piece of paper, so you may more easily refocus students' thinking on the task when necessary. More advanced students may want to and should be encouraged to do their own writing.

The purpose of this brainstorming is to help participants—students and tutors—clarify their own thinking. They have come up with a task, something very specific that they want to accomplish in their writing, and the brainstorming session helps them focus on what they want to do, what they want to say, how they want to say it, and to whom and why they plan to write. Together you are using the spoken language in a very meaningful way, as together you seek to tackle a task, to solve a problem.

THE WRITING PROCESS

1. **SELECT TRIGGER EVENT**

2. **PREWRITE**
   A. DISCUSS
   B. SET THE WRITING TASK
   C. BRAINSTORM

3. **WRITE**

4. **READ AND RESPOND**

5. **REVISE/REWRITE**

6. **EDIT/REWRITE**

STEP 3. WRITE

The students write to get a first draft of the brainstorming ideas.

The student or the group has figured out what to say and how they want to say it. Now the tutor says, "Our task is on the board. We've brainstormed about what we want to say. We even have some of the key words written down. Let's fill out the writing to get all our ideas down on paper." Encourage the learners to write the best they can; if they cannot spell a word, have them write as they think it might be spelled, or write the first letter and draw a line (d_____). Assure them that no one else will see their writing.

Because new writers can have difficulty in concentrating on all aspects of the written language at one time, experience and research show that you postpone discussion of editing procedures (spelling, capitals, punctuation, verb forms) until students have drafts on paper. You want writers to concentrate first on getting their ideas down in writing. After writers have written something, then you can go back and look at grammar and mechanics.

You may still have a reluctant writer; in fact, you may be a reluctant writer yourself. The students have talked through their ideas already so it may be helpful for you to say, "We said it. Now we can write it."

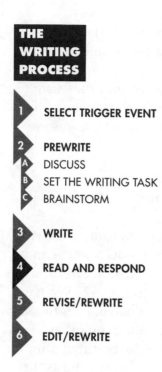

THE WRITING PROCESS

1 **SELECT TRIGGER EVENT**

2 **PREWRITE**
A DISCUSS
B SET THE WRITING TASK
C BRAINSTORM

3 **WRITE**

4 **READ AND RESPOND**

5 **REVISE/REWRITE**

6 **EDIT/REWRITE**

STEP 4. READ

The students read the written material out loud to help clarify what they have written.

In this step, writers will serve as their own audiences as they read for review what they, as well as their peers, have written. Writers should read their work silently and then aloud to themselves; then they should read to the tutor, writing partner, or small group. Reading aloud can be intimidating at first, but it is important for several reasons:

First, it shows students the close relationship between reading and writing.

Second, most native English speakers know when something does not sound right. We might not understand exactly why, but our ears are trained through life experiences to know what "sounds right."

Third, as listeners to our own reading—and readers of our own writing—we become more aware of audience, and we can catch and correct things that don't sound right to us.

To promote discussion after listening, you can establish this routine for both one-to-one and small group tutoring: Ask each person to make at least one positive comment on the writing and pose one clarification question to the writer. Sample questions include:

♦ What did you mean by . . . ?

♦ Could you tell me more about . . . ?

♦ Could you describe . . . ?

♦ What happened after . . . ?

♦ Is there anything else you'd like to add . . . ?

THE WRITING PROCESS

1 SELECT TRIGGER EVENT

2 PREWRITE
A DISCUSS
B SET THE WRITING TASK
C BRAINSTORM

3 WRITE

4 READ AND RESPOND

5 REVISE/REWRITE

6 EDIT/REWRITE

STEP 5. REVISE/REWRITE

Writers now go back to the draft to make changes in the writing.

The writers go back to the piece of writing and make changes, usually to answer the questions from their own, the tutor's, or their peers' reviews of their writing. Students might need to add details, use stronger verbs, put things in a logical sequence, add descriptive words, or delete repetitions.

Revision generally concerns content or structure whereas editing deals with mechanics (spelling, punctuation, etc.). If the students are working on a computer, this revision process is very easy, and every copy—first draft, second draft, final product—is indeed a printed page. If not, you might have students write in pencil or on every other line of the page. That way, they can easily add words, phrases, or sentences without too much trouble.

For various reasons, the revision stage of the process is often the one at which the students respond slowly. Remember that the actual physiological act of writing is sometimes painful to students who have never developed the fine motor skills used in writing. Erasures are often messy. The students can be embarrassed by the appearance of their work. Reassure the new writers, letting them know they can rewrite a little later if they "mess up" their pages by revising them. The difficult part is getting their ideas on paper, and they've already done that.

STEP 6. EDIT/REWRITE

The editing step in process writing helps each student work on the "skills" part of writing that proficient writers have command of. This step also helps you tailor your instruction to each student's needs.

In this step, the writers pay attention to grammar, usage, and the mechanical aspects of writing (spelling, capitals, punctuation, etc.). Even with a three word sentence by a very beginning writer, for example, the focus could be on

THE WRITING PROCESS

1 SELECT TRIGGER EVENT

2 PREWRITE
A DISCUSS
B SET THE WRITING TASK
C BRAINSTORM

3 WRITE

4 READ AND RESPOND

5 REVISE/REWRITE

6 EDIT/REWRITE

beginning a sentence with a capital letter or capitalizing the first letter in a proper name.

Don't spend much time on editing in early lessons. Writers are often sensitive about errors, and they need encouragement to write. Even suggestions for improvement can be construed as criticism, so tread softly. People may mistake discussions about the errors in their papers for attacks against their personalities. Since many people are frightened of exposing themselves on paper, you want to defuse their fears. Look for patterns of errors and note them in your students' assessment portfolios (folders of selected writing samples, attendance, books and stories read, etc.).

Editing is the most sensitive part of this cycle. As the writers become more confident, they will be better able to deal with constructive criticism. Remind your students that every writer has an editor, sometimes himself, sometimes another person. The amount of editing may depend on the intended audience. For example, a letter to the Board of Education should be as nearly perfect as possible. Something written for one's own use could be more casual.

After a few sessions, encourage writers to be their own editors. Encourage members of the small group to ask each other questions about spelling, grammar, usage, and punctuation.

Keep copies of each student's writing in individual portfolios. After each session, go over your notes. These will help you plan individual practice and activities for each writer. Note the length of the written pieces as well as the frequency and the types of errors made. Note also the positive aspects of the writing: nice use of details, good organization, clarity of expression, etc.

For your purposes as a tutor, look at student writings to see patterns of strengths as well as needs. Refer to the questions in Chapter Eight on assessment of writing. Your assessment of student strengths and needs should guide your instruction. If you find, for example, that a writer has a particularly strong ability to structure an essay into logical order, note this in the writer's portfolio. If not, you can discuss structure or organization of ideas with the student and suggest that the student do some work dealing with organization in class or for home practice. If you see that spelling is not a problem for a particular writer, make that note in the student's portfolio and don't assign extra work on spelling. If you see that the student uses capitals but uses them erratically, note this pattern in the portfolio. Then, work with the student on capitalization in the part of the lesson devoted to reinforcing activities or assign work for home practice.

Be careful not to overwhelm a new student with too many corrections. Work on the most obvious problems. For example, if the student writes a paragraph with every single verb form used incorrectly, work on verbs, not every other error in the paragraph. Students may see writing as a punishment. You want to help change that attitude. While grammar and mechanics are certainly important to the process, they are merely one step. We don't expect our students to become proficient readers overnight; neither should we expect them to become proficient writers overnight.

Students writing on the computer can have a final draft in a matter of minutes. If your students do not have access to the computer, your typing the final draft gives students a boost. When texts are typed, they look more like the print students see in books. If you don't have access to a computer or a typewriter, then write the texts carefully in manuscript. Of course, you can also suggest students recopy their own final drafts.

At least monthly, discuss each writer's progress using examples from the portfolio. It's encouraging, for example, to say, "Mario, your first writing was three sentences long. Look how much more fluent you have become in your writing. You wrote a half-page on this latest project. You're really making progress."

CHECKLIST ✔

The Writing Process

1. Select Trigger Event

2. Prewrite

   a. Discuss

   b. Set the Writing Task

   c. Brainstorm

3. Write

4. Read and Respond

5. Revise/Rewrite

6. Edit/Rewrite

We have discussed this process as it relates to tutoring in general. Below is a very specific discussion of how you can use writing in a lesson on goal setting. You and your students will work collaboratively in order to determine the students' goals.

USING THE WRITING PROCESS IN A LESSON ON GOAL SETTING

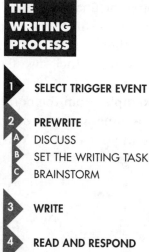

THE WRITING PROCESS

1 **SELECT TRIGGER EVENT**

2 **PREWRITE**
  A DISCUSS
  B SET THE WRITING TASK
  C BRAINSTORM

3 **WRITE**

4 **READ AND RESPOND**

5 **REVISE/REWRITE**

6 **EDIT/REWRITE**

STEP 1. SELECT TRIGGER EVENT

In this example, the trigger event is the topic of setting goals. You can start the lesson any number of ways. You could introduce the idea of individual goal setting by using printed materials that reflect literacy learners' goals. One story available is "My Goal," by a literacy learner from Kentucky. (This story appears in *Slices of Life: Kentucky Writers for Kentucky Readers*, published by the Lexington, Kentucky, *Herald-Leader*.)

You might want to read the story aloud to your student or group. In "My Goal," the author writes that she entered a literacy program for one reason: to read a book to her daughter. Her daughter, who is now in her twenties and has her own child, used to walk around the house, carrying her favorite little book, *The Bunny Rabbit*. When she was little, she'd climb up in her mother's lap, dragging the book with her. Her mother, a nonreader, would point to the pictures and make up stories.

In time, as the little girl started school and became a reader herself, she stopped climbing into her mother's lap, demanding to be read to. No words ever passed between mother and daughter about the subject.

After the daughter married, the mother entered a literacy program. Her goal? To read to her child. On Easter Sunday after the mother had been in a program for over a year, the daughter, now expecting her own baby, came home for a visit. Based on the story, we can imagine that their conversation went something like this:

"Go back in your room and get me your favorite book," the mother said.

"Is it time for me to take it home with me to read to my own baby?" asked the daughter as she returned to the den with *The Bunny Rabbit* in hand.

"No, I plan to keep that book," was the mother's reply. "Here, now, you sit in my lap." The daughter looked at her mother incredulously. "I'm your mother, and I say sit in my lap," repeated the mother. Laughing, the daughter obeyed.

The mother opened the book and began to read, "Once upon a time . . . ." Mother and daughter both burst into tears. After a few minutes, though, the mother asserted herself: "We've got to cut this out. I have waited 25 years to read this book to you, and I intend to do it!"

**THE
WRITING
PROCESS**

- SELECT TRIGGER EVENT

- PREWRITE
  - A DISCUSS
  - B SET THE WRITING TASK
    BRAINSTORM

- WRITE

- READ AND RESPOND

- REVISE/REWRITE

- EDIT/REWRITE

STEP 2. PREWRITE

STEP 2A. DISCUSS

After you read or tell the above story, tell the student or the group that the story is true. Then ask, "What did you think of it?" Allow a few minutes for discussion. Encourage reactions to the story.

Then ask, "What was the mother's goal?" Students will probably say, "To read to her little girl" or "To read the book about Peter Rabbit." Then you could say, "As we begin our sessions together, we must figure out our own goals. This woman had a very specific goal that she wanted to accomplish. Her tutoring sessions focused on that goal. What are some of the goals you'd like to accomplish in our time together?"

The trigger event was the story of a mother accomplishing her goal. Encourage the students to discuss some of their goals.

When working with a group to set goals, consider which of the two kinds of groups you are working with: those formed around an announced topic or focus (such as reading with children or improving job performance) or those formed without an announced topic (e.g., you have three people who may not even know each other and want to meet to learn to read better as a small group on Wednesdays and Fridays). The session on goal setting will differ accordingly. The group formed around an announced goal can go right into setting the writing task, Step 2b, after a short discussion to remind everyone of the purpose of the lessons.

Whether you are working with one or several learners, your purpose is the same: to get students talking about goals. You might ask students for a definition of "goal" if you find that they initially have trouble with the concept. This discussion should take only a few minutes, although it is perfectly acceptable to go five or ten minutes, as long as the discussion is focused on goals.

STEP 2B. SET THE WRITING TASK

Summarize what has been said.

Tutor: "In our discussion, we've said there are several goals we'd like to accomplish. We all said we wanted to read and write better. John said he'd like to make more money. Elise said she'd like to talk to her children's teacher without being embarrassed. Marita said she'd like to read better. For this session, let's concentrate on some very specific things we'd like to do."

"Remember the woman in the story? Her goal was to read one specific book to her daughter. Tell me what your goals are and I'll list them on the board, unless you'd like to write them yourselves."

When working with only one student, encourage that learner to be specific on a goal.

Write the task and the discussed goals on the board, a flip chart, or a piece of cardboard or notebook paper. The students should see the words describing the task written down.

STEP 2C. BRAINSTORM

The tutor and students have discussed goals earlier. That discussion was rather broad, concerning the writer of "My Goal," other people they know, and possibly themselves. Now it's time to narrow the discussion to focus on the writing task at hand. Suggest that each participant identify a specific goal.

Your job is to help the students clarify or narrow their goals into manageable short-term goals. For example, it's common for some learners to say, "I just want to learn to read better." Ask, "What do you want to learn to read better? Is there something at work you'd like to read? At home? Some kind of hobby?" Continue to explore their interests and needs.

You might have students who have stated they would like to go into formal adult basic education classes and work toward a high school equivalency diploma. Be sensitive to their feelings as you respond, "That's certainly a worthwhile goal. It might take you a little time though, several years maybe. Let's make that a long-term goal. What would be a specific goal you'd like to accomplish within the next few months that might eventually lead to a diploma?"

Examples of learner goals are listed in the Appendix on pages 158-159. These can help you as you try to help the students clarify or narrow their individual goals. Do not read lists to the learners; use these examples as suggestions. Lists should not be used as menus. Often, adult learners will fall into the old school mode of choosing one of those items on what they consider "your" list rather than telling you what they really want to do. Again, ask, don't tell. Keep probing through open-ended questions to help students explore or articulate their goals.

If you're working with a group formed around a topic, the group goal is easier to discover: read to children, read the newspaper, get a driver's license, etc. Suggest that group members take two or three minutes and tell at least one specific goal each has set.

It's up to you to set closure on this activity. Give the learners a time limit to keep them secure.

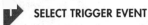

THE WRITING PROCESS

SELECT TRIGGER EVENT

PREWRITE
A DISCUSS
B SET THE WRITING TASK
C BRAINSTORM

WRITE

READ AND RESPOND

REVISE/REWRITE

EDIT/REWRITE

STEP 3. WRITE

After students have articulated their particular goals, the tutor should summarize, signaling the next step.

Tutor: "We've shared our goals. Let's take a few minutes and write down at least one or two specific goals."

If the learners are hesitant, assure them that no one else will see their writing without permission. Restate the goal, emphasizing that the students have already talked, now they just need to write.

Here is an example of how one tutor handled this situation.

Tutor: "Marita, you said you'd like to read the inventory items at your work station. You said the words. Now write those words."

Marita: "How am I supposed to spell *inventory*?"

Tutor: "What else could you call them? What else could you say? 'My goal is . . . ?' Finish that sentence another way."

Marita: "My goal is to read the things at work."

Tutor: "Great. Now write what you just said, 'My goal is to read the things at work.'"

STEP 4. READ AND RESPOND

Suggest that the students read their goals silently. Then ask for volunteers to read their goals aloud.

You will probably want to list your students' goals on the board or on paper. It's a good way to let the students see (and then "read") their goals. You have two options: you can have each student read to you and you write the goals on the board, or you can ask for volunteers to write their own or others' goals on the board. Since this goal setting activity should be done at the first or second tutoring session, it may be less threatening to have them read to you and you write. But, of course, ask, don't tell. You may have someone who likes to write.

THE WRITING PROCESS

1 SELECT TRIGGER EVENT

2 PREWRITE
A DISCUSS
B SET THE WRITING TASK
C BRAINSTORM

3 WRITE

4 READ AND RESPOND

5 REVISE/REWRITE

6 EDIT/REWRITE

89

It's important to discuss the goals as they appear on the board. Clarification questions should be encouraged. Be sure to reinforce students' work with positive comments. Questions that might bring positive responses could be: "What are particularly clear points?" or "What makes this very easy to understand?"

Learners sometimes select goals that may take a year or more to reach, such as earning a high school diploma or getting a better job. Sometimes they select broad, hard to measure goals such as being a better reader. In these cases, as you respond you might ask the students to help word the goals in such a way that they are more easily measurable and/or attainable. Help them focus by asking direct questions. Suggest they write down something they can see or do. For example, you can't see "a better reader" but you can see someone "reading two books." You can't see "a better job," but you can see someone "reading a want ad."

THE WRITING PROCESS

1. **SELECT TRIGGER EVENT**

2. **PREWRITE**
   A. DISCUSS
   B. SET THE WRITING TASK
   C. BRAINSTORM

3. **WRITE**

4. **READ AND RESPOND**

5. **REVISE/REWRITE**

6. **EDIT/REWRITE**

STEP 5. REVISE/REWRITE

Encourage the learners to write more or to play around with what they have already written based on the discussion of goals. This is not a tremendous undertaking because you have asked for only two or three goals. With the words already on the board, learners can correct their own spelling if they wish. Each student has now said, read, and written the words, explaining goals. You have written them correctly as an example.

This is an early session. You might not want to elaborate or further develop the goals. You might want to add comments on the board or easel paper, but not on the individual learner's papers. You might see that the learners have had enough writing for the day. While elaboration or development provides expanded practice with the learners' own writing about goals, use your own developing knowledge of your students to decide when to go to the next step.

If you are working with beginners and asking them to write, one sentence is usually enough. If your learners are more advanced, you probably will get more writing. Let them decide how much to write. The earlier procedure of sharing, commenting, revising, sharing, commenting, and perhaps revising further is then repeated as learners produce their texts:

♦ Learners read their sentences to the group (one-to-one learners read to their tutors).

♦ The group comments. Then the tutor comments and asks clarification questions.

♦ Learners revise based on the comments.

- ◆ Learners again read to the group (or to the tutor).
- ◆ The group (or one-to-one tutor) again comments.
- ◆ Learners may or may not revise further.

You can stop at this point if you or your students seem tired or tense. Be encouraged that the students did some writing.

THE WRITING PROCESS

1 ▸ **SELECT TRIGGER EVENT**

2 ▸ **PREWRITE**
A ▸ DISCUSS
B ▸ SET THE WRITING TASK
C ▸ BRAINSTORM

3 ▸ **WRITE**

4 ▸ **READ AND RESPOND**

5 ▸ **REVISE/REWRITE**

6 ▸ **EDIT/REWRITE**

STEP 6. EDIT/REWRITE

The purpose of this first or second session has been to set goals for future sessions. You may not have time to do any more editing or rewriting at this time. You have written the goals on paper or on the board. Students may have corrected their own spelling at Step 5 or they may do so now. Students should be encouraged to copy their goals in their notebooks for further reference. The tutor should also copy the goals for individual files.

Remember to keep a portfolio (folder of selected writing samples, attendance, books and stories read, etc.) for each student. Ask each individual student to make a copy of his or her goals for your portfolios. Students keep the originals and give you the copies.

USING THE WRITING PROCESS WITH A BEGINNING LEVEL STUDENT

You can use this writing model with a very beginning level student as well as with an advanced student. Consider the following example:

STEP 1. SELECT TRIGGER EVENT

The trigger event starts the discussion. In this example, Chuck Meadows walked into his first tutoring session and said he wanted to learn to read and write to pass a test at work.

STEP 2. PREWRITE

STEP 2A. DISCUSS

The discussion in this case centered on the test. The tutor discovered that Chuck had dropped out of school after five years because he had to work. The tutor asked him to write his name and address. He wrote his first name but asked the tutor to write his last name. He was unsure of how to write it. The tutor asked, "Chuck, are you unsure of writing or spelling your last name?" "Both," Chuck replied.

At this point, the tutor knew that the written part of the test at work was probably not going to be a realistic goal for Chuck to accomplish in the near future. She also sensed that if Chuck could set and accomplish some smaller goals, he might feel better about himself.

STEP 2B. SET THE WRITING TASK

The tutor helped Chuck set the task: "Why do you want to pass the test? If you could tell me why, maybe we could set some short-term goals."

STEP 2C. BRAINSTORM

The task was set in the form of a question; the brainstorming centered on answering that question. Chuck explained that he could not be promoted unless he could write reports about the various work stations in his area. He had been at his job for ten years: he worked hard, everybody respected his knowledge, but he couldn't read. He could not write either. He could not even write his last name.

STEP 3. WRITE

Ordinarily, after the tutor had discussed goals with a potential student, that student would have been asked to write the goals and the writing would have been saved in the student's portfolio. After Chuck had revealed to the tutor he couldn't write his last name, the tutor decided that would not be the best approach. Instead, the tutor asked him, "If you could write anything, what would you write?"

Actually, the tutor thought Chuck would say he'd like to write his whole name. However, Chuck's response was, "Chuck Meadows is a mighty good worker."

The tutor and Chuck made seven word cards, with each word in the sentence on its own card. Chuck could spell three of the words: *Chuck*, *is*, and *a*. The tutor spelled the other four words as Chuck wrote. Then, the two practiced making sentences with the words, using the word cards:

> Chuck is a worker.
> Chuck Meadows is a good worker.
> Chuck is a mighty good worker.

Chuck wrote these sentences in his notebook, transferring each sentence from the word cards.

STEP 4. READ AND RESPOND

Chuck had said all the words, he had generated the sentences, so now he read his sentences aloud. The tutor asked, "Do you want to say more?" Chuck replied, "Not today I don't."

The tutor's response to Chuck was that she was proud he had done so much at the first lesson. She also called attention to the fact that "Meadows" had been included in the sentence, so Chuck could practice writing his entire name now.

STEP 5. REVISE/REWRITE
There was none in this situation.

STEP 6. EDIT/REWRITE
The tutor called Chuck's attention to capitalizing the first letters of proper names. This editing lesson was appropriate since two of the seven words were names.

USING THE WRITING PROCESS WITH A GROUP OF INTERMEDIATE STUDENTS

Four intermediate level reader/writers, maintenance workers in the Bates Garment Factory, were requested to write a report to their supervisor. The management was working to improve the company by setting quality management standards, involving all the departments. They needed the help and suggestions from these custodial employees.

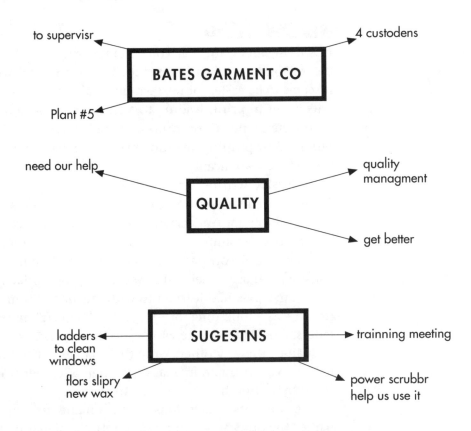

Discussions and brainstorming brought the following key words, with their own creative spelling. Mapping expanded their ideas.

All four group members talked. One man volunteered to draft. He also volunteered to read the first draft to the group. For their second draft, they decided they needed more details.

Because the report had to be sent that day, the workers asked the tutor to correct the spelling on the second draft.

No other help was given. The tutor typed the report, which was sent to the supervisor as follows:

To the supervisor
Bates Garment Company, Plant #5

We are happy to help the plant get better by getting quality management. We are 4 custodians and we need more ladders to clean the windows. The floors are slippery. We need new wax and a power scrubber. Show us how to use it. And we want more training meetings.

Thank you,
Bill Morgan
Roger McMann
John Anderson
Roberto Herrera

HANDWRITING

It is most important that you be familiar with both manuscript and cursive writing before you start to teach students. We usually start with manuscript writing because it seems to be easier for new writers. It also resembles the letters the new readers will encounter in print, leading to a situation in which reading and writing reinforce each other. Since most forms and applications require that the person filling them out do so by printing, learning manuscript writing provides learners with a practical, immediately applicable skill.

Cursive writing may be taught after your students have learned manuscript writing. In cursive writing the letters are connected. Sometimes this connectedness is helpful to poor readers who have trouble keeping a word together. To teach yourself the two recommended alphabets, practice manuscript and cursive alphabets using the sample on page 163 as a model. Remember these are models only: be consistent to use upper and lower case as appropriate.

Sam Davis had learned to write his name in manuscript as he learned the letters. It was a milestone for him and he "signed" most of his papers with manuscript letters. One day he came with a specific request. Would the tutor teach him to write his name "the way others write their names"? The tutor had not felt Sam was ready for cursive writing, but "ready" is when a learner really wants to do something. So she showed him how to connect the letters.

As he worked laboriously on his name, he explained that when he signed his name "the other way" (in manuscript), the signature was sometimes questioned and often needed to be verified. It was embarrassing. But even more important, next week was the PTA meeting, and he wanted more than anything else to be able to "sign in" as the other parents did.

What if a student has no interest in learning cursive? That's fine. Do not be surprised to find that your students will progress at a faster rate in reading than in writing. And do not keep your students back in reading because of an inability to write or spell all the words in that lesson. Keep moving ahead in reading, but continue practicing the writing used in earlier lessons. Writing is also an excellent way to review a lesson.

SPELLING

Because spelling is important to writers, you may want to teach it in some portion of your lessons. For a detailed plan for help in spelling, see the Appendix for *Spelling and the Adult Learner* (pages 184-187). However, the words to be spelled correctly which come out of your students' writings are most appropriately learned during home practice. Students need to know that they will have to practice spelling individual words if they want to really "own" those words.

When students are unsure of how to spell a word, suggest that they write it as they think it should be, or write the first letters followed by a line (sp_____) so that they don't lose their train of thought. As they review their work and want help on a specific word, how can you help?

When students ask for help in spelling a specific word, you could suggest that they:

1. Write the word one or two different ways to see which one looks right. Seeing it written down often triggers a correct spelling (*deep, depe, deap*).

2. Spell the word aloud to check which spelling sounds right.

3. Think of another word in the same pattern, rhyming with the word. (*Bright*, the problem word, rhymes with *sight*. If they know the beginning letters, *b*, *r*, and know that *sight* ends in *-ight*, they may come up with the correct spelling.)

4. Refer to other print material to see how it is spelled.

5. Look it up in the dictionary. If the students have no dictionary handy and if trial writings and spellings fail, you can always give the correct spelling.

6. Ask other members of the group. A real change in attitude occurs when group members begin to see each other as resources.

As one way to help your students gain ownership of a specific word, you might suggest that they write it several times, with intervening attempts to recall the correct spelling following this model:

1. Say the word while looking at the word spelled correctly.

2. Write the word, saying it while writing.

3. Cover the models and write the word again, saying it while writing.

4. Refer again to the model. If the word is correctly spelled, cover the model and write the word again. If spelled incorrectly, refer again to #1, 2, and 3, looking for syllable breaks or patterns, and checking until the spelling is correct.

5. After a lapsed time, perhaps 10 to 15 minutes, write the word again. If it is correctly spelled, the word is probably known. If it is incorrect, some type of review would be indicated.

Sometimes your students may need to have correct spelling at once. They may be writing letters or reports that must be mailed that day, and they don't want the embarrassment of incorrect spelling. Just as the spell check on a computer gives instant correct spellings, you can give your students the same help. While you don't want to intimidate students by pointing up every incorrectly spelled word, you must honor their requests for instant help as well.

One way to give the correct spellings when requested by the students, yet let the writers retain the right to change or not change those words, is to underline each misspelled word carefully and put a number above it. On another page, not on the text, write the correct spelling of each word with a corresponding number.

The students then have the option of rewriting their text correcting spelling. These misspelled words, too, give a personal word list which can be reviewed for spelling in a later lesson.

You might want to give students a chance to indicate those words they think are not spelled correctly. They might have their own ideas of strategies to correct the spelling. In small groups, students often help each other with spelling.

Spelling can be an independent area of learning for students, or it can be part of your work together. You may want to suggest that your students develop a personal spelling list.

CONCLUSION

As you think about writing and the tutoring of writing, consider the following:

♦ Your definition of writing might not be the same as your students'. Writing is primarily the creation of a text for a particular purpose and audience. It also includes sub-skills and editing skills like handwriting, grammar, spelling, and punctuation.

♦ You may or may not go through a whole writing cycle with every student at every session. The important thing is to include some reading, some writing, some listening, and some speaking at each lesson. You will see that most students learn faster when language components are presented in an integrated rather than an isolated manner.

By the same token, not all writing needs the same degree of revising and editing. One would revise a grocery list to make sure all items are included, but would probably not correct spelling or rewrite for neatness. One would be more careful and detailed about a story to be submitted for publication.

♦ Students may say they don't need to know how to write. What do you write? Novels, poems, plays, short stories? Maybe not. How about notes, appointments, lists, letters, checks? That's writing also. In a learner-centered situation, you will want to help students identify their own writing needs.

♦ Many programs are publishing student writings. Seeing one's own words in print in a bound publication is a great incentive for writing as well as a boost to self-esteem. This project is especially easy if students regularly use the computer for writing at least final drafts.

♦ It is never too early to start a student on a computer. You might be concerned that the student does not know the keyboard, but the hunt-and-peck method does not distract even beginning students. Actually, using the computer has a positive effect on student self-esteem.

♦ If students are really excited about very lengthy stories but their hands cannot move as quickly as their thoughts, you might encourage them to record their stories on a tape recorder and take dictation from themselves, regulating the tape to their own speed. Tape recorders are also good for students who can say what they want to write but have a mental block once they try to put pen to paper. They, too, can record their messages and play them back to themselves.

♦ Everybody has a story to tell, and writing preserves those stories. The written word connects where we've been to where we're going; it preserves our past and looks toward our future. If we view writing in that way—rather than as a negative way to record grammar and spelling errors—our students will value it as we do.

♦♦♦

◆ INTERVIEWING THE POTENTIAL LEARNER

CHAPTER

VI

INTERVIEWING THE POTENTIAL LEARNER

EACH TUTORING PROGRAM has its own particular guidelines for interviewing students and for matching them with tutors. The kind of information collected during an initial intake interview when the potential learner either calls or comes into the literacy program's office includes name, address, telephone number, age, number of years of schooling, marital status, employment, as well as information on when and where a potential student can meet. Asking students to write their own names and addresses gives beginning evidence of their writing abilities.

The interviewer will also note why students want to improve their proficiencies with reading and writing and what their interests, needs, and goals are. The program office uses this data to help select compatible tutors for students and to give tutors background information on their students. Other forms allow the interviewer to find out more about students' interests, goals, and current reading and writing habits.

The interview is usually conducted by the program's matcher or by some other person whose role is to interview prospective learners. What is learned from this interview is given to the tutor prior to meeting with the student or small group. This program interview is an individual interview, even if the student eventually goes into a small group.

THE TUTOR'S INTERVIEW WITH A STUDENT

It is imperative to begin your tutoring adventure with a personal interview. No matter who interviews the student initially, your own interview with the student is most helpful. During this interview, you will be able to go into greater depth or ask clarification questions about information collected in the program's interview. Be sensitive about probing unnecessarily into a student's personal background. Both you and your student will be using this information to set goals and plan the kinds of materials and topics to use during lessons. Remember, the interview is as important for the student as for you.

Exercise 7:

Feelings About My First Tutoring Experience

If you've never tutored before, write down how you feel as you think about getting ready for your first tutoring session. If you have tutored before, describe how you felt before you met your first student.

♦♦♦

Thinking about your first tutoring session may make you a little nervous. That's understandable. Inexperienced tutors generally are afraid that their failure to do everything perfectly will translate into the student's failure to learn to read and write.

You must be conscientious as tutors, of course, but fortunately you're not required to be perfect. Your most important qualities will be an expectation that your students will learn, patience to be realistic about the rate of learning, the ability to recognize students' strengths and needs, and the willingness to plan. A good rule to follow is be prepared with student-centered lesson plans and with student-selected materials, but also be prepared to go with the flow, to change plans as needed.

PURPOSES OF THE TUTOR'S INTERVIEW

The tutor-student interview should accomplish at least five objectives:

1. Acquaint the tutor and student.

2. Establish a positive rapport.

3. Provide an informal assessment of each student's literacy skills.

4. Help each student continue to articulate and/or clarify personal goals.

5. Assist each student and tutor in planning the course of instruction.

AN EXAMPLE

Jo Smith came to a local literacy program and said she wanted to get her high school diploma. The intake interviewer found that Jo had attended seven years of school before dropping out because she "couldn't read words." Turning to one of the word lists in the back of **TUTOR**, the interviewer asked Jo to read a few words. Jo attempted three or four words, miscalling them all. Based on the discussion with Jo and further assessment, the interviewer knew Jo was a very beginning student.

The intake interviewer matched Jo with a tutor, to whom this information was given. The tutor called Jo to set a time for a "get acquainted" session or interview before the first actual lesson. Keeping in mind the purposes of the interview, the tutor set about to learn more about her student: to find out more specific goals so they could use these goals around which to plan their tutoring sessions together.

Notice from the following conversation that the tutor helped Jo articulate some more easily achievable short-term goals:

Tutor: "I see you'd like to work on your high school diploma. A high school diploma is a wonderful goal but it may take quite a while. If you could tell me why you'd like to earn your diploma, maybe we could set some short-term goals. Why would you like to earn your high school diploma?"

Jo: "So I can do better on my job and read the Bible."

Tutor: "What do you need to read at work?"

Jo: "Well, I want to come to work through the front door. I can't tell which door is mine because I can't read the sign that tells which is the Morris Dining Hall."

As they continued to talk, the tutor found that for the past few years Jo had used the back door to go to her job in a cafeteria, located in the basement of one in a row of several buildings which all looked alike. She was petrified to go to the front of this row of buildings in the fear that she could not read the sign directing people to the "Morris Dining Hall" and would be left to wander aimlessly around the area.

Once at work, she was constantly humiliated as patrons ordered "whole wheat," "lite wheat," "white," and "lite white." She could only identify bread by the color, so if she chose the wrong one, she was met by jabs like, "I said lite white. Can't you read?"

The conversation further revealed that Jo attended Bible study every Sunday night. She had a lesson book, but she could read so little of the lesson that she rarely attempted it, although she badly wanted to participate in the discussion.

The tutor was able to make the following suggestions:

Tutor: "Jo, we'll make sure you get help as you start work on your high school diploma. Right now, though, I hear you say that you've got three other important goals. You want to read the sign 'Morris Dining Hall,' read the labels at your work station, and read your Bible lessons."

Jo: "That's right. I didn't know you'd help me with those things. I thought you'd only help me go to school."

Tutor: "Of course we'll help you with those things. And remember, any reading and writing you do now will eventually help you when it comes time to work on your high school diploma."

The tutor asked Jo if she'd like to write the goals in her notebook. Jo declined, so the tutor wrote them. Remembering the theme of immediate relevance, and since reading "Morris Dining Hall" was not an overwhelming task, the tutor proceeded with a short lesson.

The tutor and Jo made three word cards: "Morris," "Dining," and "Hall." Writing, in this case, was not even in sentence form. The tutor wrote each word on a sheet of paper, and Jo copied them on 3" x 5" index cards.

From her three word cards, Jo was taught to read "Morris Dining Hall." The *Hall* part was easy, because she knew the word *all*. She knew the sound of *h* and thus could fairly quickly master *hall*.

"Dining" was next. She could read *-ing. Di-* looks like it sounds, especially if the *i* says its name. Next, the *n* was added to *-ing*. Then, she read *di-ning*.

"Morris" could have been more difficult to teach, but the tutor didn't let it seem difficult. Jo knew that McDonald's started with *M* (the *M* of the golden arches is great to use with low-level readers). She knew the sound of /*m*/ for *McDonald's* and for *Morris*.

Then the tutor did something a little different. The two walked to the front of the row of buildings that included the Morris Dining Hall. Jo was invited to find the sign with the cafeteria's name on it.

As they stood looking at these buildings, the tutor asked her some problem-solving questions:

Tutor: "How many words are we looking for? Which word do you want to find first? What will be an easy clue?"

Jo found the building, and the two walked inside, Jo finding other signs for Morris Dining Hall as they made their way to the cafeteria. Jo, of course, was delighted. She had experienced a success!

Notice what the tutor did in this interview. She listened to the learner's goals, asking clarification questions. Focusing the student on setting and meeting more immediate short-term needs and goals, the tutor still affirmed the student's long-term goals. She provided concrete information about the program and what it could do. Finally, the tutor helped the student experience immediate and relevant success.

As you probably realize, students often have difficulty stating a specific short-term or more easily realized goal. Note the long-range goals but concentrate on the short-range goals that can be accomplished much quicker. In this way students will feel that sense of satisfaction needed to keep the desire alive to continue in the program. In this example, the tutor focused on a short-range goal articulated by the student. Through the tutor's asking, not telling, in the interview process, the focus for the learner-centered instruction surfaced quickly.

SUGGESTED ACTIVITIES FOR FIRST MEETING

Meet and exchange telephone numbers and addresses. Decide on a time and place to meet. Perhaps bring a calendar for each student, jotting down the time and date of the next meeting. Decide what you prefer to call each other: Mr., Mrs., Miss, Ms., first names, or nicknames.

EXPLAIN THE TUTORING PROCESS

Explain what types of exercises might be included in a lesson. For example:

Tutor: "Let's use materials that you are interested in as part of the lessons. We'll do a variety of exercises, learn words you need to know, read together, and do some writing."

Encourage your students to bring any reading material they find difficult and would like to be able to read, such as school notices, doctor bills, or newspapers. Suggest that each student bring a folder or notebook for class work (unless you plan to furnish them).

SET GOALS

Review individual student intake interview forms, refreshing yourself on goals. Ask general questions to expand on the information given to the program interviewer. You might continue with the reading and writing assessment activities as described in Chapters Four, Five, and Seven.

Write down a long-term goal and some short-term goals you've agreed upon. Have the students write these goals or give each a written copy. Use the writing process in Chapter Five to develop a few sentences focusing on students' goals.

Continue discussion, asking questions, being sensitive to student needs, interests, and goals, as well as to strengths and weaknesses.

◆◆◆

◆ RESOURCES AND ACTIVITIES

CHAPTER

VII

RESOURCES AND ACTIVITIES

ONE OF THE FIVE THEMES OF THIS BOOK IS IMME-DIATE RELEVANCE; as you provide activities students find relevant, the tutoring sessions will be more productive.

Learning to read and write can be a challenging and satisfying series of successes as you accommodate your students' needs, interests, and capabilities, sensing when to change materials and when to nudge the learners.

The advantage of tailoring tutoring to students is that the students are not committed to a prescribed curriculum. They are spared the necessity of learning material that may be tediously irrelevant to their lives. Your challenge is to locate materials of interest to your specific students.

Because it's rare to find materials for adults neatly categorized into grade levels, we prefer to look at broader groupings that allow for such factors as students' prior knowledge, language, and interests. This chapter will look at resources and materials relevant to the abilities and needs of students.

RESOURCES

MAPS

If students want to read maps, find out what type of maps they have in mind. You might develop a map of the area where you meet. This strategy allows you and the students to use the "map" to represent a real, known area. If there is a misunderstanding about what the map represents, you have the actual space as a reference.

You and your students could walk around the park, neighborhood, city, and beyond. Gradually make the transition of using only a map, letting the students be the guides.

Planning a trip—even an imaginary one—can be a lot of fun. The names of cities and states and words for road signs and directions are all practical words constantly needed. You might capitalize on your students' interests in a certain place. You might provide the students with a series of directions that could be followed only by the use of a standard road map. In addition, using the mileage charts on maps can be an interesting way to incorporate some math for your students.

A city map can provide an additional source for map reading skills. Your students can identify what streets would be traveled to reach the airport, a shopping plaza, or the library.

CALENDARS

Using a calendar is a valuable skill. First, students need to understand what a calendar is and how it can be used. When students know how the days of the week are noted at the top, you can explain why the first day of the month is sometimes a Sunday, sometimes a Monday, or another day of the week.

Remember that learning occurs by doing. Talk with your student about important dates to remember. Practice using the calendar to note meetings, birthdays, doctor's appointments, rent payments, or pay day. A pocket calendar or a page-size monthly calendar simplifies keeping various commitments. Suggest that students write down the days and times of your lessons and other important dates.

MENUS

In your constant search for practical materials, don't overlook menus from restaurants, cafes, or diners in the area. You might bring in a few, or ask the students to bring some. Encourage the students to read what they can from these menus. Ask students what they like to eat or what they would like to order. Then teach these words from the menus. You can teach some words as sight words (e.g., *pizza, soup*); teach others by associating them with words already known (e.g., *beef stew, hot dogs*), applying the principles of word patterns.

OTHER AUTHENTIC MATERIALS

Recipe books, food boxes, product labels, health and safety folders, magazines, song lyrics, sales circulars, and travel brochures—all print around you and your students is fair game for lessons. Have students bring in material that they are interested in reading. In this way they can exercise some control over the content of their lessons.

GAMES

Games can be valuable tools that bring a change of pace to lessons and give the students an opportunity to use the strategies they've been working on. Whether you use games that you purchase or that you create, keep in mind that any game should:

1. Involve reading and writing.

2. Be fun and challenging without frustrating the students.

3. Be geared to adult interests and abilities.

4. Be played fairly. (Do not allow your students to win if they don't deserve to.)

As with many other materials, adapt games to fit the needs of each student. Don't worry about changing the rules; remember that materials are there for your use. Simple crossword puzzles, either from books or devised by you, are fun to do with students. Incorporate words the students are having difficulty with, or perhaps put their own names into the puzzle.Commercially available word games include *Anagrams, Scrabble, Spill n' Spell, Boggle,* and *Scattergories.*

You might invent trail games, letting the students set the destination. Names of cities could be included; road signs (STOP, DETOUR) could be deterrents, and other signs (SPEED LIMIT 55, THRUWAY) could move the traveler more quickly.

A challenging but entertaining way to work on word recognition is to play Word Bingo. On letter-sized sheets of paper or cardboard, draw appropriate lines and write in manuscript some words your students are working on, making each sheet different by mixing the arrangement of the words. Write the same words on a set of cards from which you and your students will draw. Take turns pulling the word cards and reading them as you cover the word on the sheet.

WORKBOOKS

If workbooks are used, it is important that they not be mechanically worked through page by page, book by book. Instead, always keep your students' goals in mind, interspersing reading and writing events as often as possible.

TAPE RECORDERS

A tape recorder can be an excellent educational tool, and many students have them. If not, perhaps students can check out tape recorders from your program. They can read aloud with a taped presentation and follow the words in a book outside the lesson. Following along with a taped reading provides a model of fluent oral reading and accurate word pronunciation. Students can review material and repeat activities as they please. This lets students have the responsibility for some self-evaluation.

If your students don't know how to use tape recorders, show them. Then encourage them to work independently. Be sure to record the date and the students' names on each tape, keeping records of this information in their portfolios.

Here are some other ways tutors have found to use the tape recorder as a tool:

1. Record your students as they each read aloud. Have the students play back their tapes. Each student often spots reading problems and seeks to correct them.

2. Find out what kind of music your students like. Use lyrics as a tool for learning to read and write by getting copies and suggesting that the students read or even sing along with the tape.

3. Make an audio recording of a selection your students find interesting. Provide them with a written copy of the selection. Have each replay the selection, reading along with the tape. This exercise will improve the individual's fluency in reading.

4. Tape a sample of the student's oral reading as you are assessing each student's progress. Recordings taken at intervals give you a permanent record for later referral and evaluation, and provide evidence of student progress.

5. Tape an entire lesson with you and your students. At your leisure, listen to the tape and critique yourself. Are you talking too much? Do you sometimes talk down to your students? Do you give them enough time to respond to questions?

A note of caution. Preview any material before you use it with students. Regional accents, loud music, and childish intonation on some commercially-produced recordings make them inappropriate for use with adult students.

Using a tape recorder can be fun and can give you a change of pace in a lesson. It will help give your students confidence in their own abilities as they hear their own improvement.

COMPUTERS

There is much excitement about the use of computers in teaching basic reading and writing. Many hesitant writers do not balk at writing on the computer for several reasons. First, poor handwriting often deters writers. Physically, writing can be difficult, even painful, for new writers who may not have developed the fine motor skills needed for neat handwriting. Second, revising and editing are much easier to do on a computer than by hand. They do not require nearly the physical effort needed to add details and re-copy, edit and re-copy. Third, the printed page is pleasant to any reader's eye. New writers often become discouraged and embarrassed because of handwritten papers, which can appear messy. Fourth, spell check programs provide another way to reinforce spelling. Finally, the ability to write on a computer is a real boost to students' self-esteem.

Using computers for writing should not replace teaching students to write by hand. Everyone has access to a pencil or pen. Most of us are given forms to be filled out on the spot. We all make lists. Certainly you should work on the formation of letters with students. If you and your students have access to a computer, though, don't hesitate to try it, especially when students will be working on writing that will require revising and editing. Making printouts at various stages in the development of a text will allow students to see their actual progress.

Do not think you need to teach handwriting and computer writing at different times. You can begin these two things at the same time. Students do not need to form letters beautifully before they begin to write on the computer. If you are not familiar with computers, you and your students can learn together.

If your literacy program doesn't have a computer, look into using the facilities of a local library, corporation, school, university, or public adult basic education program to see if they would share their computers and their word processing or teaching programs during the "off times."

There are several books available that give detailed directions for using regular word processing, spelling checkers, and spreadsheets to teach reading and writing in an authentic environment.

ACTIVITIES

NOTES AND LISTS

Notes and lists may be two of the most frequent ways writing is used in our day-to-day living. Discuss the kinds of notes that the students would like to write, then ask each to write a few notes. You will likely get a note to a family member, a shopping list, a list of activities for the day, or a note to a teacher.

JOURNAL WRITING

Of the many types of journals, we'll discuss three—private, dialogue, and circular. They are used for different purposes.

PRIVATE JOURNAL WRITING

Private journal writing appeals to many learners. And it's just that, private. Your students may or may not want you to read what they write. Even if they ask you to read it, make comments or suggestions only on the content, not on the mechanics. Private journals are for each individual student's use. Ask your learners to write at least two sentences a day in a special notebook. They can write about what they did that day or how they felt about the day. They can make comments about the weather or experiences with a friend or family. As students progress, encourage them to write

109

more. Often these two daily sentences will expand to a page or two. Point out that writing—any kind of writing—is also going to help them with reading. Rereading their journals may give them ideas for further writing.

DIALOGUE JOURNAL WRITING

In this type of journal, you also write, responding to what the learners have written. The process continues back and forth. This dialogue leads the learners to rethink and expand on what they have written. Your response will serve as a model for correct grammar, spelling, and punctuation. Reading what you write further develops the learners' language and comprehension skills.

Even very beginning readers and writers are able to use a dialogue journal. The first entries may include pictures or brief written messages. You can respond by writing a nonjudgmental comment. As you write, keep your students' reading proficiencies in mind.

CIRCULAR JOURNAL WRITING

Journal writing also can be used to write fiction. The tutor starts a story, finishing with a cliffhanger-type sentence, giving it to a student to write the next part. When the student finishes, it goes back to the tutor or other students in the group, and they continue to add on to the story. The tutor, of course, models correct usage and spelling. It's fun, and, for some students, more comfortable than private or dialogue journals because it isn't about their personal lives. Again, over time the students become more creative and write longer passages.

LETTERS

Letter writing can also be a valuable experience for students. Perhaps you are going on a trip. You can continue your lessons while you are away by writing to your students. Write in manuscript or cursive, depending on the ability of your students, and use words your students know or can figure out. You might also send postcards to your students when you are away. Sending postcards lets people know that you remember them. Postcards also carry a simple personal message that students can read, as well as a picture of a part of the world your students may not have seen.

Suggest that students write to you as well. The first time, it's a good idea to give your students a pre-addressed envelope and a sheet of paper showing how to write a letter. In your lesson, demonstrate how to start a letter and several ways to end a letter.

Writing letters to out-of-town friends or family members can also be motivating and meaningful to many students. One student began corresponding with his grandmother whom he hadn't seen in fifteen years. It not only meant a great deal to him but also provided authentic reading and writing material for lessons.

A personal letter could be:

Dear Mom,

We got to Detroit the first night no trouble with the car weather is great Will
write more tomorrow

Love,
Richard

One student wrote a more formal letter to her child's teacher:

Dear Mrs. White,

Please send Sharons glasses home today call me if you need me

Yours truly
Mrs Beverly Jackson

You will get a big thrill when you receive your student's letter. It might be the first letter your student has ever written. The spelling may not be perfect, the grammar may not be correct, but you'll know what it means, and that is the important thing.

ALPHABETIZING

Alphabetizing can be a helpful skill when using a phone book or a dictionary or when searching for a book in the library. Most people can recite the alphabet from memory; if your students cannot, write the letters in order as an easy reference. Explain that dictionaries, telephone books, and files are set up in alphabetical order.

Use a variety of words your students may need to alphabetize, perhaps selecting ten names that start with the first ten letters of the alphabet:

Don	*Alice*	*Carl*	*Gus*	*Frank*
Beth	*Edna*	*Harry*	*John*	*Irving*

Put each on a word card and have the students put them in alphabetical order. You could use animals, flowers, or cities, depending on your students' interests. When your students can alphabetize words beginning with all 26 letters, point out that:

A through *F* would be roughly in the first third of the dictionary.

G through *O* would be roughly in the middle section.

P through *Z* would be roughly in the last third.

This guide will be useful as a quick reference for dictionaries.

Some students do not realize that words are put in alphabetical order using the second or third letters when the first or second are the same. Suggest that your students alphabetize the following words: *as, apple, about.* Then have them alphabetize words for which the differing letter is the third one: *bread, bride, brain.* Continue to point out opportunities to alphabetize as they occur in your sessions.

ADDING NEW VOCABULARY WORDS

How do you add new words to your vocabulary? Do you refer to a list of unknown words, disciplining yourself to look up the meaning of five new words a day? No, most people usually add to their vocabulary just by living in a world in which language is used. Even as you read for fun, you don't stop and look up the meaning of each new word. You're too intent on the story; you can't stop. And by the time you've read that new word two or three times, the meaning has usually become clear. You've added a new word to your vocabulary.

Just so with your students. They automatically add to their vocabulary as they read. If, however, the meaning of a word doesn't become clear in the context of the reading material, suggest that they jot down the unknown word and guess at the meaning. Then they can look it up in the dictionary to see if they were right.

LIBRARY USE

Students may be introduced to the public library early in tutoring. You might want to check it out first to locate the adult new reader section.

Since libraries can be intimidating to some new readers, it is a good practice to make a library visit a part of your lessons. During the first visit, help students get library cards and become familiar with the library's services. It is a good idea to provide or arrange a tour of the library and to point out the variety of materials available. For example, many adults don't know that public libraries have videotapes; recordings; reference, business, voter registration information; and special programs for both children (story hours, movies, and summer reading programs) and adults (movies and speakers). Some libraries even loan framed prints and toys.

During your library tour, review check-out procedures including how to determine when the book is due and how to renew a checked-out book when you need more time. Users of libraries must know that there is a fine for overdue books and that they are responsible for books checked out on their cards. It may be possible to work out an arrangement with the library to allow extra renewals or longer borrowing periods for adult new readers.

Let students know that it is unnecessary to finish a book they don't like. Share some situations in which you have started a book but lost interest in it or found it inappropriate for your own needs. Let them know that you can't judge a book by its cover and that many people initially misjudge books.

Unless there is a special collection of books for adult literacy students, it will be extremely difficult for a low-level reader to find usable books from the confusingly large volume of material available. If your library does not have a special collection for adult beginning readers, urge them to establish one. Ask the librarian to help the students find appropriate picture or simple reading books.

One way to help students through this maze of materials is for tutors to locate several books related to each student's goals and interests. You can help students choose a book by looking at author, title, illustrations, information about the author, chapter headings, length, etc. Since not nearly enough nonfiction has yet been written specifically for adults with lower reading proficiencies, the next best resource is juvenile books. The usable juvenile materials are not usually listed in the bibliographies for adult beginning readers, but students tend to be enthusiastic about them. If your program doesn't have a list of these titles, you may have to go on a treasure hunt in the juvenile's book section. To make certain the material is appropriate, read a little yourself and check the illustrations. Be sensitive; avoid going into the children's section unless the students express a desire to do so.

The method of locating books in a library is changing. Instead of a card catalog, there may be microfilm or a computer that the librarian will demonstrate for you. No matter which method is used, you can locate a specific book by author, title, or subject.

Many students and tutors meet in libraries for their lessons. As students begin to feel comfortable in libraries, they enjoy exploring the different sections. Encourage their exploring.

SEQUENCING/FOLLOWING DIRECTIONS

Even for someone with limited reading skills, you can use sequencing skills. Ask your students to respond to two or three verbal directions. For example:

> "Open your book to page 62, and count the number of words in the first five lines."

Something as simple as this exercise can give you information about whether a student can follow directions. It also enables you to determine whether students understand the boundaries between words.

Gradually increase the number and complexity of the directions to which your students are asked to respond. For example:

> "Open your book to page 25. Look at the pictures and then tell me what you think the article is about. After that, let's jot down the key words together."

As a practical exercise, to reinforce aural sequencing, give your students a series of directions typical of those offered to a person seeking to find a particular house:

> "Go up the hill past the third traffic light. Turn left at the Exxon station, and go to the white house with the red mailbox in front."

See if your students can repeat these instructions in order. Encourage your students to develop a picture in their minds as they listen. This helps to increase the likelihood of following the directions in the right order.

Then move to printed directions. Recipes and how-to-do-it manuals are good sources for practice. The directions on a cake mix box are excellent. Have your students read through the entire sequence of action and then describe or act out the sequence required by the directions. They can refer to the printed directions at any time. The purpose is to keep the directions in the correct sequence.

Another interesting activity is to take a strip of paper and write down a sequence of events:

In the morning when the alarm clock goes off, I have to get up, get dressed, eat breakfast, and catch a bus before 7:30.

Cut apart each phrase containing one activity or description, and ask your students to reassemble the events in order. You might find a different sequence, for one student might suggest:

When the alarm clock goes off in the morning, I have to get up, eat breakfast, get dressed, and catch a bus before 7:30.

Another way to practice sequencing is to cut apart the panels of a comic strip, asking your students to reassemble them so they make sense. This activity often requires careful attention to visual details as well as to the words quoted.

Look around you. You'll find many commercial products that can provide additional skill practice in following directions and in sequencing.

SILENT READING

It is often suggested that adult new readers be given material below their reading level. This practice has many advantages, including building the confidence of new readers as they read right along without stumbling. It also allows for comprehension, not just reading word by word or calling words. However, at times you want to challenge new readers, to encourage them to push ahead, to let them know that they are capable of reading and understanding more than they realize.

One tutor, leaving on an extended trip, was trying to prepare the members of her small group for more independent work. The two students read at approximately the same level. The tutor looked for material at a higher reading level. The subject matter had to be interesting and sufficiently tantalizing for them to want to read on. She got the *Readers Digest's* version of *Jonathan Livingston Seagull* and gave each of them a copy. They looked at it and immediately said that it looked too difficult.

The tutor suggested that they read the first two pages silently. Afterwards, they were to tell what they'd read. Almost immediately, one student asked the tutor what one word was, since he couldn't sound it out, he didn't know it by sight, and it didn't look like any pattern he'd had. She asked him just to skip it, and read along. She thought he'd get the idea.

Shortly, the other asked for help on another word. The tutor again suggested skipping the word. After several attempts to get the words from the tutor, the students shrugged their shoulders and continued reading.

When they both looked up, finished, the tutor asked them what they had read. Speaking sometimes together, sometimes alternately, they retold the story.

Discovering they could comprehend without reading every word was a revelation to them. They talked about it. They then realized that they could read more than they thought they could.

The trio continued. The tutor read part of the story aloud to them (she wanted to be sure they saw reading for enjoyment, too), and the students followed, reading silently. The session stopped at a crucial point in the story. The tutor said they were free now to read or not to read the rest of *Jonathan Livingston Seagull*. Both students asked to take the book home. They had confidence to read even beyond their self-set standards.

You as the tutor must know when to give reading material below readers' levels and when to challenge them with material beyond their levels. High-interest material that challenges learners to stretch is another element of reading that shouldn't be overlooked.

SUMMARY

Often motivation can be maintained and comprehension enhanced by varying the materials. Games, maps, calendars, letters, tape recorders, and computer-assisted instruction can all be used to reinforce learning. But if your students have not been motivated by any of these suggestions, perhaps their rate of learning can be improved by a more structured approach. In all cases, be patient, be flexible, be creative, and be aware of your students' reactions to the learning/teaching taking place.

Be sure that new learning is firmly based on what your students already know. Don't limit yourself to the suggested motivational materials and activities given in this book. Invent a few of your own!

Volunteer tutors constantly come up with new, creative ways of teaching. Reading is a partnership among tutors, librarians, family, friends, and students. To teach literacy skills successfully you must provide practical, planned instruction using materials meaningful to your students. And you must do it in a relaxed, accepting manner.

♦♦♦

115

◆ **ASSESSMENT AND LESSON PLANNING**

CHAPTER

VIII

ASSESSMENT AND LESSON PLANNING

LITERACY LESSONS should begin instruction focused on each learner's expressed needs. *Instruction* should yield *assessment* information which should be used to develop plans and/or refine existing plans.

From this point of view, assessment is the close examination of a student's progress toward his or her own goals. The evidence of that progress is in the collected records and work samples of the student's reading and writing. *Assessment* is the process of collecting and reviewing the information, whereas *evaluation* involves the judgments made about the quality of the work. Progress, then, is noted as there is evidence of positive change in the quality of the samples collected.

FORMAL ASSESSMENT

Most formal assessments are designed to measure students' progress with specific reading and/or writing strategies and skills. However, a majority of these tests were developed for children and are inappropriate for either teenagers or adults. To fill the need for an easily administered tool for adults, Ruth Colvin and Jane Root developed **READ: Reading Evaluation Adult Diagnosis** (rev. 1999, New Readers Press), which provides for the measurement of the following competencies:

1. Basic sight word recognition.

2. Specific word analysis skills in relation to:
    Names and sounds of letters (consonants)
    Blends (*bl, br*)
    Word patterns (*mat, sat, fat)*
    Reversals (*was* for *saw)*
    Variant vowels (vowel sounds other than the short vowels).

3. Level of reading ability (word recognition in context).

4. Levels of reading and listening comprehension.

Information from **READ** will help you decide which skills need reinforcement and what portion of your lesson should be devoted to each skill. You could also use the results, which give approximate levels of reading and listening comprehension, as a general guide in developing lessons and selecting materials.

Of course, **READ** is just one of the many measures you can use. Check with your coordinator to find out which measures are used in your program. Whether you use the **READ** or other evaluation instruments, you should know that a reading level is a rather nebulous concept. A score used to determine a reading level on any test should be looked at as a ball park range and not as the definitive answer about a particular student's ability.

GRADE EQUIVALENTS AND READABILITY FORMULAS

Much of the material available for both instruction and testing is given a "grade level" difficulty ranking. The grade level is most often determined by the use of one of many readability formulas. Be careful not to rely solely on readability formulas to measure the suitability of a particular title for adult new readers. Readability formulas focus on such things as number of words and syllables, sentence length, and use of word lists. No readability formula measures such key factors as a reader's prior knowledge or interest in the topic.

Since readability formulas cannot be viewed as entirely trustworthy, it follows that graded materials used in testing can't be viewed as yielding hard and fast grade equivalents for students either. A beginning student who has difficulty with the nonsense language used in many Dr. Seuss books may have greater success with a note she has written (or dictated) to her child's teacher even though the note may contain several multi-syllabic words that can't be sounded out. A student with more proficiency may find reading the driver's manual a challenge but have no trouble with the sports page of the daily newspaper. Some more advanced students may do very well on test items but may find it difficult to read and retell a simple short story. By the same token, of course, many good readers may have to reread the text of legal contracts or insurance policies.

Reading is more than just learning to pronounce words and marking the correct answers. The more experience or prior knowledge students bring to the print on a given topic, the more control they are likely to have over that print. Readers use all the clues available to them: the print on the page (letters, sounds, words); the context of the language in print; their own experience and knowledge of the topic; and their own vocabulary and language proficiencies. Therefore, the more of these clues present, the less difficult reading becomes. The fewer the clues, the more difficult the reading.

We prefer to look at proficiency in reading as broad ranges of ability rather than as narrow grade levels. For our purposes in this discussion, the following will apply:

Proficiency Range	*Traditional Grade Equivalent*
Beginning	0 to 1st grade
Early Intermediate	2nd to 3rd grade
Intermediate	4th to 5th grade
Advanced	above 5th grade

INFORMAL ASSESSMENT

If you need to measure student progress for a program or funding agency, you will want to do some type of formal assessment. However, for weekly tutoring sessions, to show specific accomplishments and to help you plan your lessons, you might find more informal, easy-to-do assessments helpful.

PORTFOLIO ASSESSMENT

Keep samples of your students' materials in folders or portfolios. A student-centered, multi-measure portfolio assessment includes:

1. Writing samples.

2. Notes on student's strengths and needs.

3. List of student's long-term and short-term goals.

4. Record of materials read.

5. Record of student's attendance.

6. Personal word list.

7. Progress reports.

8. Student's self-evaluations.

These various records are kept by the tutor in a folder. Students may want copies of the records for their own folders, which they may keep at home or bring to the tutoring session. However, the tutor should keep a folder for each student.

At regular intervals—at least monthly—tutors and students will want to review the folders. Together you can review the materials read, read early writing samples and compare them to later writings, and mark off goals attained. This review is a great motivator for students and a practical way of record keeping for you.

INFORMAL ASSESSMENT OF ORAL READING

A tutor can find out a great deal about a student's reading by listening to the student read aloud. As students read aloud, listen for patterns and make mental notes of answers to these questions:

1. Do students hesitate before each word?

2. Do they consistently miscall certain letters or words?

3. Do they read word for word instead of in phrases?

4. Do they read with intonation in their voices, using their voices to denote questions, commands, or dialogue?

5. Do they pause at the end of a sentence?

6. Do they stop at the end of a paragraph?

7. For words that are miscalled, is the problem one of misreading (*cow* for *could*) or one of seeing one word and calling it a similar word (*house* for *home*)?

8. Do students catch themselves when the words they read do not make sense? (Do readers say, "Oh, that doesn't make sense" when they read "I was so sick I cow not eat my supper"?)

Listening for answers to these eight questions as students read will help you plan instruction. If students hesitate before reading each word, you will want to work on fluency. Perhaps the text is too difficult for them. If they consistently read beginning *br* blends (*brick, bring*) as simple *b*, you'll want to work on words beginning with *br*. If they don't hesitate at the end of a sentence, you'll want to let them know that a period signifies a pause.

120

The above suggestions deal with students' abilities to correct themselves, to "self-monitor." Proficient readers know when they have read words that do not make sense in a sentence because they are constantly monitoring their own reading. You will want to help new readers understand that these monitoring activities are necessary for fluent reading. You will also want to help new readers develop these self-monitoring strategies. Your notes on the student's oral reading, included in your copy of the student's portfolio, will give you good information from which to plan instruction in your lessons.

INFORMAL ASSESSMENT OF WRITING

When viewing student writing, you might want to look for several things. As we discussed with assessing oral reading, you want to look for patterns. You will base some of your instruction of skills on the needs that show up in the students' writing. Let these questions guide you as you make notes for each student's portfolio:

1. Fluency. How much do students write? Does the text seem to flow?

2. Structure. Does the text have a structure? Does it narrate; describe; give a sequence; go through the process; give examples; list reasons, causes, effects; state a problem and offer a solution? Or does the text seem to ramble on with no apparent sense of organization?

3. Vocabulary. Do students vary use of vocabulary or do they constantly use the same words over and over again in their writing? Do they use vocabulary appropriately? Is the vocabulary concrete (words you can "see"), or do they use vague pronouns and linking verbs (*is, are, was, were*)?

4. Development of Ideas. Do students explain key ideas, using examples or details? Or do they expect the reader to read their minds?

5. Syntax (word order within a sentence). Do all sentences follow subject and verb pattern or do the students vary their sentence structure with introductory phrases or clauses?

Are there any irregular placements that English speakers don't generally make (for example, "the doll little" instead of "the little doll" or "to running" instead of "to run")?

6. Mechanics and Usage. Do students have trouble with spelling, subject-verb agreement, pronoun agreement, verb forms, pronoun forms, punctuation, or capitalization? Do students write incomplete sentences (fragments) or run several sentences together with commas or no punctuation?

OTHER KINDS OF ASSESSMENT

Before proceeding with instruction, watch for indications of any difficulties the learners appear to have in eyesight, hearing, behavior, or learning.

SIGHT

Do students squint, read with one eye covered, tip their heads so that the bridge of the nose obscures the vision in one eye, hold the book too close or too far away, rub their eyes, or complain of eye fatigue? Each of these symptoms suggests a referral to a vision specialist. Many areas have organizations that will provide free glasses.

HEARING

Must learners look at you to be sure of hearing what you say? Is one side or another favored while listening? Do you have to repeat things often? Do they speak loudly even when there are no other noises to distract the listeners? Any of these symptoms may suggest a hearing screening is needed.

OTHER

You may also encounter learners who have other problems that may not be easily identified by casual observation. Such learners may have great difficulty in linking the words they see with the words they speak. These individuals may be quite bright yet be very difficult to teach to read. Because of the technical nature of these difficulties, we will not try to deal with them here. If progress is so slow that both you and the learner are discouraged despite the best efforts, teaching may have to be discontinued or modified. Some adults need specialized and intensive instruction (more than two hours a week) to learn, and some rare adults will remain nonreaders despite all efforts to teach them.

If you encounter a suspected sight, hearing, or other problem, inform your program staff as soon as possible so that appropriate action can be suggested.

USING ASSESSMENT FOR LESSON PLANNING

In the remainder of this chapter, you will be given instruction on how to translate learner-centered goals and your assessment of each student into objectives for learning. You will learn how to plan lessons that, while flexible, progress in a logical manner toward accomplishment of each learner's short-term and long-term goals.

EXAMPLE 1: A LOW-LEVEL READER/WRITER

Mark is a learner in a small group of fathers organized around the topic of reading to children. His long-range goal is to get a high school diploma. His short-range goals are to read children's books to his children and to help them with their homework. Mark has little confidence in his reading and no confidence in his writing ability. He reads at a lower level than any other father in the small group and has recently begun one-to-one tutoring in addition to the small group.

In planning Mark's one-to-one instruction, his tutor works closely with the small group tutor, who keeps records of which books the small group has chosen. The majority of instruction in Mark's one-to-one lessons is directly related to the particular book the group is reading at the time. These lessons have included assisted reading and work on comprehension in addition to word attack skills.

In his second tutoring session, Mark was excited about reading a child's book. He worked with his tutor in an assisted-reading situation. Immediately after reading the book, the tutor asked, "What did you like about that book?" This question sparked a lively discussion.

Mark made his own word cards from five words in the book, but he also wanted to make word cards of his children's names. He and the tutor worked on word patterns formed from *look* (a word that appeared several times in the text of the child's story) and *book,* using the list in the Appendix of *TUTOR* to get other patterned words (*cook, hook, took*).

Mark and his tutor decided that a notebook in which Mark would keep a summary of the plots from the various children's books would be a help when the family went to the library. However, when the tutor suggested that Mark write a few sentences about the book they had just read, he balked. "I can't write," he said. The tutor assessed the situation.

"We've talked about the book. You like it because . . . " and the tutor recounted what Mark had said.

"I just can't write," Mark repeated.

"Mark, if you could write anything, what would it be?" asked the tutor.

"I think I'd like to write a letter to my mom about the kids," Mark replied.

Mark, like many other students, was frightened of writing. Because the tutor found what Mark wanted to write, they had a base for starting the actual writing. The point is that the tutor assessed the situation and planned instruction related to Mark's goals.

USING GOALS TO PLAN LESSONS

A long-term goal is a destination—the distant city, the far mountains. Short-range goals are the sign posts along the way that help measure progress toward the ultimate goal.

But before you set out on such a journey, you need to analyze just what you have to do to reach your destination. This task analysis results in a list of things that must be known or done if the goal is to be reached. The translation of goals into objectives is much like making a list of things to do before you take a trip:

◆ Pack the car.

◆ Get money from the bank.

◆ Put gas in the car.

If one of your student's goals is to use a telephone book competently, your list of objectives might look like this:

- ♦ Alphabetize names through three letters.

- ♦ Use guide words on the page.

- ♦ Alphabetize first names.

- ♦ Explain abbreviations used in a phone book.

- ♦ Find categories used in the yellow pages.

- ♦ Find other sources of information in the phone book.

The practical result of task analysis is the setting of an objective for a particular lesson. What you and each learner will want to accomplish by the end of the lesson determines what you'll teach. For example, if a student wants to be a cook, a short-term goal could be to collect recipes. Being able to write and then to read a recipe could be the objective for one lesson. The recipe could provide the unifying objective for the majority of the activities during that lesson.

While this selection of a theme is helpful, you need not restrict yourself to keeping everything in a single theme. You could do some free or silent reading or discuss cooking or nutrition with your students rather than sticking with recipes throughout the whole lesson.

IDENTIFYING APPROPRIATE MATERIAL

Student interest is of primary concern in planning lessons. It is important that your students be involved in selecting books and other materials that will be used for either instruction or for recreational reading.

Bring several books to class or take your students to the library. Encourage them to look for books of interest. In directing your students' selections, point out the various things to look for when selecting a book. Ask the students what the cover tells. Ask them to look at the chapter headings, the table of contents, and the introduction. Have them look at the pictures or illustrations and skim the book, reading random sentences and paragraphs. If working with a small group of learners, you may want to have them work in pairs, examining and discussing which book to choose.

Ask your students to choose among several books you think will be of interest. Have each student read a few paragraphs silently. If any student thinks it's too difficult, have him/her look at other books until an appropriate book is found.

THE LESSON PLAN

You and your students have identified a short-term goal and specific objectives that lead to that goal. You probably have a good idea what skills you want to work on, based on your prior work with each student.

After you choose the topic, select the skills to practice, the materials required, and the instructional activities. Your lesson planning will then follow naturally and will be composed of the following parts:

1. Assessment.

2. Instruction.

3. Evaluation.

Feel free to allow student performance during the lesson to determine what skills you cover. For example, you have listened to students read. You have seen their writing. You have planned a lesson based on their interests. You want to talk, read, and write about that topic. You have planned to work on word patterns. However, as this lesson progresses, a student writes a 5-sentence paragraph with no capital letters. In this situation, you might want to concentrate on capitalization in the lesson.

To design a successful lesson that assures progress, you must first know:

1. What interests your students.

2. What the objective of the lesson is.

3. What your students already know.

Informal reading inventories and structured questioning will give you information about each student's interests and what she or he wants to learn to read. But you must listen and observe carefully to gather information about how each individual learns best.

Some adults learn better if they talk aloud to themselves. Others will learn best when they write. Some learn with only a few practice sessions. Others need dozens of repetitions to remember things. Some will use a newspaper for practice, but will not use a workbook. Others prefer structured workbooks. Some love to work on a computer; others are frightened at the thought. These strengths and needs, likes and dislikes, must all be considered in a program tailored to individual learners.

EXAMPLE 2: A TYPICAL LESSON

As you and your students plan together, a typical lesson could include:

1. Review of Previously Learned Material and Homework. Few of us can master a new skill or a new task with only one explanation or trial. Your lessons contain many concepts that must be reviewed and practiced many times before they are learned thoroughly. Confidence is built as mastery is completed.

Don't be misled into thinking that all review is boring to students. Although it may seem repetitious to you, remember that this material is new to the students. Review cements skills and concepts in the minds of students.

125

Begin lessons with a short review of material already, or nearly, mastered. This provides your students with needed maintenance experience and gets the lesson off on a positive note. Home practice should also be reviewed and evaluated to demonstrate to students that working on their own is a vital part of learning to read and write. To assure progress, it is crucial that your students practice and apply the new skills between lessons.

2. Reading and Writing. Chapter Five, "Writing," describes in detail the selection of the topic in the lesson. While students will probably not produce a rough draft and revised paper in every tutoring session, the discussion of topic and trigger events is helpful as you seek to plan lessons. As you plan each lesson, write down the objectives on your lesson plan. For example:

◆ Read all the words on an employment application.

◆ Sequence correctly the steps in repacking a faucet.

◆ Write a letter to a child's teacher.

As you teach, break the skills into steps small enough to be thoroughly mastered and reinforced in a relatively short time, a lesson or two in most cases.

Adjust your plan as you go along. Each lesson provides the basis for planning the next lessons. Language experience stories give insights to learner interests; samples of reading and writing reveal strengths and weaknesses in word analysis and comprehension; writing samples reveal strengths and indicate needs for instruction in spelling, punctuation, grammar usage, and vocabulary.

Remember that mastery in one lesson does not guarantee long-range mastery. You'll be reviewing some material in the same session in which you'll be introducing new concepts. If, despite repeated exposure and simplified objectives, little mastery seems to have been attained, drop the activity and return to it later when it will seem new again, when it seems more relevant to the student.

3. Reinforcing Activities. Included in each lesson will be combinations of discussions for comprehension, assisted reading, writing, practice on needed skills, and reading for pleasure. And you'll want to include everyday activities to reinforce the lessons learned. For example, you can work with games, maps, calendars, letters, tapes, notes, computers, newspapers, and puzzles, as described in Chapter Seven.

4. Assignments for Practice/Homework. Homework assignments should be planned with the students and should be part of every lesson. Your students may not respond to this easily, so try to make it interesting and appropriate, explaining why it is important. Reading and writing achievements will often be slow if they must be acquired with only two or three hours a week of involvement. Reading and writing must be exercised to be acquired or maintained. No one learns to read or write without practice, and it is the learner who must provide the practice. Don't even imply that reading and writing can be taught during the lesson time alone.

Make it easy to take work home. You could write short homework assignments so then your students could even work on homework during coffee breaks.

Home practice will vary depending on the needs and abilities of each individual student as well as the work done at that particular session and the time each student has to commit. Learners could:

◆ Take a copy of their writing home to reread every day.

◆ Practice word cards from their personal word list.

◆ Read a page or a chapter from a library book every night.

◆ Read for ten minutes every day and keep a record of what is read.

◆ Write in a journal three or four times a week, even if each writing consists of a sentence or two.

◆ Prepare a meal following a recipe.

◆ Make a list of things to do or items to buy at a store.

◆ Play a word game with a family member.

◆ Fill out a sample application for a library card or bank account.

◆ Write a message on a postcard and mail it to a friend.

◆ Circle all the *m*'s on a newspaper page to review the sound or see the letter in everyday use.

◆ Read the words on a menu from a local restaurant.

◆ Work on the computer at the library.

The possibilities are limited only by your own imagination and that of your students. To become a better reader and writer requires frequent reading and writing. Two sessions a week will not provide sufficient practice time for meaningful progress to take place. Therefore, it is imperative that students understand that between-lesson practice is crucial to learning to read and write.

5. Reading for Pleasure. As you try hard to teach students all the skills involved in reading and writing, be sure to let them know that reading is pleasurable. Use the last five or ten minutes of your lesson to read aloud to your student or group. You could read a short article on football, ecology, or fashion. Try some poetry or a short story if they reflect your students' interests. Don't ask questions.

You could tape any of these readings for the learners to review at home, thus extending the lesson time. Planning a final few minutes of reading aloud emphasizes that reading can be fun.

6. Wrap Up. At the end of each lesson, discuss your students' feelings about the session. Find out if there is anything they would have liked to do more of or anything they didn't like. Decide together what the objectives of the next lesson will be. Get their ideas for what they'd like to read next.

After your lesson, write notes about your students' progress on the day's lesson plan. Sometimes you can do this during the lesson; however, if your note-taking interferes with your students' concentration, do it after the lesson. Comments, evaluations, and future plans as agreed upon should also be written down immediately after the tutoring session.

The objectives of the next lesson will depend on your students' performance, interests, and needs. They will help you decide on techniques and materials to have on hand. Be sure students participate in the evaluation of the lesson. Ask what they enjoyed or found difficult. Be open to any suggestions the students may offer. Review progress often so that each student can see achievements. (See pages 192-193 and 194 for sample lesson plan forms.)

CHECKLIST

Planning a Lesson

1. Assess and Review. As you plan for the next lesson, remember to assess and review your notes from the current lesson plan.

2. Overplan. It is better to have too much planned than not enough. The excess goes over into the next lesson, or you may want to skip some planned activities in favor of others.

3. Overteach. When your students can retain something for a period of at least three lessons, you may assume that it is learned. Don't panic when what you thought was learned seems to have been forgotten. Re-learning will come faster than the original learning.

4. Be Flexible. Many a good lesson on paper fails to work well because a learner is upset, circumstances intervene, or some other part of your plan took longer than you had anticipated.

5. Be Positive. Encourage your students, but be honest. Guarantee some success with every lesson.

6. Be Efficient. Make your plans carefully. It is the best way to assure that you will be relaxed yet alert to the needs of your students. Note successes as well as needs on the lesson plan during lessons.

SUMMARY

Careful planning and common sense are a good combination. As you gain experience, you will learn to use the techniques, shifting from one to another easily as the occasion demands. You will be able to use them with both the materials you and your students develop and with published material. On-the-spot intervention requires a skilled tutor who can assess and adapt immediately. That comes with practice.

◆◆◆

◆ TUTOR READINESS EVALUATION

CHAPTER

IX

- ◆ **ATTITUDES**

- ◆ **TUTORING STRATEGIES**

- ◆ **ASSESSMENT AND EVALUATION**

- ◆ **LESSON PLANNING**

- ◆ **CASE HISTORIES**
  Student 1: Mr. B.
  Student 2: Mr. P.
  Student 3: Ms. V.
  Student 4: Mr. J.
  Student 5: Mrs. E.

CHAPTER NINE

TUTOR READINESS EVALUATION

BEFORE YOU BEGIN TO INSTRUCT A STUDENT, you should be able to evaluate your attitudes as well as the information and the skills you will need to provide successful instruction in teaching basic reading and writing.

This chapter is a self-check to help you assure yourself that you either know information or instruction skills directly or that you know where to locate that information in this book.

ATTITUDES

1. Are you free of critical attitudes toward teenagers and adults who cannot read or have limited reading and writing skills? Do you really understand the problems? Your answer requires absolute honesty in examining your own attitudes toward those who have reading/writing limitations. See Chapter Two.

2. Are you willing to be patient with small gains and with the necessity for a long period of instruction before the goal of functional literacy is attained? See Chapter Two.

3. Can you be enthusiastic enough in your instruction to provide genuine encouragement so that your students can experience a feeling of achievement with the many small successes which must be attained before any long-term success can be achieved? See Chapter Two.

4. Do you recognize that you as a tutor are a learner in many situations? See Chapter Two.

5. Do you honestly understand and believe the philosophy that meaning is the base of literacy instruction? See Chapter One.

6. Do you understand the changing roles of tutors and students in collaborative instruction? Are you willing to work at developing these role changes in yourself and in your students? See Chapters Two and Ten.

TUTORING STRATEGIES

1. Can you describe the basic steps in language experience? See Chapter Four.

2. What are the six steps in the writing process? See Chapter Five.

3. How do you decide whether process writing or language experience is appropriate for your students? See Chapters Four and Five.

4. Why is it important to start with oral language? See Chapter One.

5. How would you help a student create a personal word list? See Chapter Four.

6. What steps would you use to teach a consonant sound your student needed to know? See Chapter Four.

7. What are some examples of words appropriate to teach in pattern. See Chapter Four.

8. Do you know how to teach comprehension from the very first lesson? See Chapters One and Three.

ASSESSMENT AND EVALUATION

See Chapter Eight

1. When will you assess your students?

2. How will you assess your students?

3. What types of things do you need to be assessing?

4. Can you describe the contents and purposes of a student's portfolio?

5. Can you explain the relationship between assessment and instruction?

LESSON PLANNING

See Chapter Eight.

Below are the descriptions of several students typical of those who receive instruction in basic literacy. Read each case carefully noting the information given. Then jot down what you think you would do if such a student were assigned to you, answering the following questions:

1. What supplies and books would you have with you?

2. How would you find your student's strengths and needs?

3. How would you find your student's goals and interests?

4. What strategies would you use to teach?

5. From what you know about this individual, suggest a focus for beginning instruction.

6. Identify by title suitable written material for the student to read.

7. What other ways can you help this student?

8. What further assessment tools would you use?

CASE HISTORIES

STUDENT 1: MR. B.

Mr. B. is 21 years old, married, with one child. He works at a foundry and says he had four years of schooling in Indiana. He is eager but shy and gentle; very polite and cooperative.

Your personal interview and assessment showed that Mr. B. could not read one word and that he did not know the names or sounds of any letters. His reading proficiency range is beginning.

If Mr. B. were assigned to you, what steps would you take to plan the instructional strategy?

STUDENT 2: MR. P.

Mr. P. is 55 years old, single. He is an unemployed migrant worker and is in Grade 1 class in Adult Basic Education (ABE). He will continue at ABE, but he needs individual help.

He has had no previous schooling. He wants to get a job, get a driver's license, and read his school work. He is most cooperative and intelligent, however he lacks confidence.

Your personal interview and assessment showed that he reads only print from his environment, such as the names of fast food places and only the common road signs such as STOP and numbers pertaining to speed and highway numbers. His reading proficiency range is beginning.

If Mr. P. were assigned to you, what steps would you take to plan the instructional strategy?

STUDENT 3: MS. V.

Ms. V., 32, is a single mother of three small children. She works at a local garment plant as a seamstress. She went to school for ten years in a small town. Ms. V. was offered a better job but could not accept it because her reading and writing skills were at such a low level. Even first level supervisory jobs at her plant require the ability to write evaluations.

Ms. V. is eager and enthusiastic. She seems intelligent, is self-confident and cooperative. She desperately wants to learn and needs help. Your personal interview and assessment showed that she reads well at the intermediate range, but her writing is unintelligible. She is very intimidated by writing. Your personal interview showed that she wants to read to her children.

If Mrs. V. were assigned to you, what steps would you take to plan the instructional strategy?

STUDENT 4: MR. J.

Mr. J. was assigned to you but there was very limited information given. In fact, all you know is his name and telephone number as arrangements were made for your first meeting.

What will you do to prepare for this first meeting? How best can you use this hour? Jot down the questions you plan to ask and the information you plan to share about yourself.

Create your own student and describe your plan for instruction for the next meeting.

STUDENT 5: MRS. E.

Mrs. E. is a 62-year-old widow whose husband had always taken responsibility for household and business affairs. She suddenly finds herself in a position where she has to balance her checkbook, pay bills, and write letters such as canceling credit cards, transferring Social Security benefits, etc. She likes to read simple inspirational stories from religious magazines. Even though she can read well at an advanced proficiency range, she finds herself overwhelmed at what she is facing at this traumatic time in her life.

If Mrs. E. were assigned to you, what steps would you take to plan the instructional strategy?

◆ THE TUTOR-LEARNER MATCH

CHAPTER

X

THE TUTOR-LEARNER MATCH

YOU HAVE READ THIS BOOK; you have discussed and practiced approaches and techniques to tutoring; you have reviewed various case histories and have seen samples of student writing; you may have met and talked with some students during your training. You've been assigned your student or students and have some background information based on an intake interview. Now what? Your first lesson starts before you get to the tutoring site. Your first session starts with preparation.

REVIEW STUDENT INFORMATION

Before the first session, review all the information your program has available about your students. You should have the results of the program's intake interview to help you prepare for your first meeting with the learners. You will know basic information about each student's name, age, and educational background. You will have an inkling of each student's interests and a general feel for individual reading ability. The literacy program's intake interviewer will give you this information. The following guidelines will tell you about the preparation you will need to do prior to the actual first meeting with the learners.

SELECT MATERIAL

After reviewing the information about your students, you will have an idea of what to bring with you to your first meeting:

1. Each student's address, phone number, and background information.

2. Name tag for yourself and students, written in large manuscript letters if working with a small group.

3. Notebook, paper, and pen or pencil for the learners.

4. A copy of *TUTOR*.

5. *READ* (or other formal assessment tool).

6. Notebook or folder for your records (attendance, lesson plans, notes).

7. Portfolios (folders) for your copy of each student's writing samples and other portfolio information.

8. Portfolio or folder for each student to keep writings.

9. Real-life reading material of high interest to the learners, e.g., sports magazines, TV guides, cookbooks, newspaper, comics.

10. Low-level, high-interest books from the library in your students' interest area.

11. Extra paper (carbon paper if you are working with dictated writing and don't have a copy machine available).

12. 3" x 5" cards.

13. Book or selection for modeled reading.

14. Beginners' dictionary.

15. Blank Learner/Tutor Agreements (see page 181) for the first session.

16. Motivational material to read to your student.

17. Your lesson plan.

OTHER HELPFUL TEACHING AIDS:

1. Clear plastic overlay to be used with felt-tipped pen on library books. (Both books and plastic can be used again.)

2. Simple crossword puzzle book.

3. Games such as Scrabble or Boggle.

The amount and variety of support equipment you will need in your meeting room will, of course, be determined by the nature of your instructional materials. A standing easel pad or chalkboard is essential when working with a group and useful with one student.

CONTACT LEARNERS

Before the first session, call the learners and impress upon them the importance of their being at the first meeting on time.

Check on a mutually acceptable time and place for the first session, making sure each student knows how to get there. You may have found space in a library, a bank's public meeting room, a community room at a mall, a church, or a union hall. Perhaps your program has a recommended list or is organized into centralized learning centers after hours at local businesses or in a space at an adult basic education program. In any case, a good place is a neutral one.

THE TUTORING LESSON

INTRODUCE EACH OTHER

It's a good practice to be at your session site before the students arrive. Sit at the table with the one-to-one student or the small group. This fosters the "we're all in this together" spirit. If it's a small group, give each student a name tag with each name written in big manuscript letters. Wear a tag with your name clearly visible too. Introduce yourself, and suggest that students introduce themselves. Give your own name, occupation, family status, hobbies, and perhaps your reason for being there. You might say, "My name is Bill Raneri. I work at the hosiery mill. I just became a grandfather last month." Your own introduction will serve as a guide for the learners as to what is expected of them.

Remind the students that the goal of the program is to improve reading and writing rather than to learn to read. Only a small percentage of the adult population is totally illiterate. The more frequent need, then, lies with those people who can read some words, but who cannot read well and, more importantly, cannot understand what they read.

These literacy tutoring sessions have two overall objectives: to improve each student's literacy performance and to help accomplish personal goals. Explain that

139

in order to keep to these two objectives, you need to know and understand what each student's personal goals are.

In a one-to-one situation, sit next to the learner. For your group meeting, a round table is desirable, but if using a rectangular table, avoid sitting at the head. This physical arrangement plays down traditional teacher-student roles and cues the learners that this is a team effort.

You have four specific objectives for that first session:

1. To get to know each other.

2. To agree on some rules that will direct the tutoring sessions.

3. To set goals.

4. To begin your tutoring experience.

ENCOURAGE PARTICIPATION

The following are strategies adopted from the *Tutor Training Manual* (1983) developed by Literacy Partners of New York City. These encourage discussion and participation of all students whether in a one-to-one or small group setting. Use them throughout the lessons.

To encourage participation:

1. Make frequent eye contact with learners to encourage them to talk.

2. Maintain a nonjudgmental atmosphere by not criticizing the opinions of the learners. Allow the learners to express their opinions before sharing yours.

3. Ask open-ended questions that encourage critical thinking and reflection (e.g., "What would you have done in this situation?" instead of "Did you like the story?").

4. Give each learner time to respond. Many tutors are intimidated by silence. If there seem to be problems, try re-phrasing the question. Avoid answering your own questions.

5. Try to paraphrase learners' comments and respond to both the feeling and content of what is said. Paraphrasing will usually encourage learners to elaborate.

6. Encourage learners to talk with each other if you're in a small group.

7. Ask learners to elaborate on what they say.

8. If you're working in a small group, create structures where learners will feel comfortable talking, such as setting tasks where the students work together outside the group.

DISCUSS RULES, ROLES, RESPONSIBILITIES

RULES

Discussing the ground rules for the sessions presents you with your first opportunity to involve students in making significant decisions. The participants will see that individual member's needs and preferences are being considered and that the democratic process is at work.

Explain that there must be a few ground rules. Suggest some, such as being on time or calling when you cannot attend, and solicit others. Encourage discussion through questioning and be careful not to suggest all the rules. Write the rules on the board. After decisions are made, suggest that the learners write their own versions in their notebooks if possible.

With a group, you might include such things as being patient with others who may be having trouble keeping up, listening to the suggestions and questions of others, making positive comments or questions, not having to read aloud unless individuals want to, allowing others to finish before speaking, and completing assignments for home practice. In a group, it will be each member's responsibility to include others in discussions as well as not to monopolize discussions. In both a one-to-one or small group format, you could start the discussion with your expectation that students will make at least one positive remark about their own writing and that any reading to be done aloud can be done silently first.

Some teams impose a "No Smoking" rule within the meeting room even if the building regulations permit smoking. Also, a two-hour session should include a ten-minute break.

If the following have not been considered in the discussion of rules, don't overlook them. Re-emphasize the importance of having everyone present at each session. Solicit reasons for attending from the students and encourage discussion of these reasons.

Give out your telephone number or that of the program office, and tell the students that you expect to be informed in advance if anyone finds he or she will be absent. Be sure you have each member's phone number, assuring them that you will call if meeting plans have to be changed. If you're in a group and they've met several times, you might suggest they exchange phone numbers in order to notify each other of an unavoidable absence or to check on homework assignments. Some tutors have found it helpful to distribute or to make calendars with the students, marking down the date, time, and place of the sessions.

One of our goals is to help students to develop into self-directed learners. You want to work yourself out of a job. In the early stage of the collaborative effort, you will be a team member, a facilitator, and a moderator. This collaborative approach applies equally in the one-to-one and small group situations. You want to transfer authority from yourself to the learners, to foster active learning, and to create a safe atmosphere based on mutual respect.

141

ROLES

Keeping the session on track may involve constantly clarifying both tutor and learner roles. In a one-to-one learning partnership, there are only the two of you. In a typical small group situation, there will probably be a tutor and three-to-five learners, for a total small group size of four-to-six members. In either situation, you and the learners must define the roles of participants to be sure that expectations can be set and met. As a tutor you have differing roles in a collaborative reading and writing situation.

Housekeeper. You or a designated person has the responsibility for:

1. Setting a time and day based on learners' schedules.

2. Securing and confirming a site.

3. Notifying learners.

4. Making name tags (at the first session if in a small group).

5. Checking the site to ensure that it is properly equipped (table, chairs, easel, pad or blackboard, perhaps refreshments).

Facilitator. After housekeeping responsibilities, you will also have to assume the roles of leader, counselor, and negotiator, even in a one-to-one situation. These same responsibilities are important in a group setting as the group forms, faces conflict and frustration, is strengthened, and finally jells.

You will find yourself taking an active role as leader during the early stages of the development of the tutoring relationship. Because this new learning situation may make some students uncomfortable, they need to know that someone is in charge. Your role will change during the life of the learning partnership. The following are some of the leader activities you will perform:

1. Call the session to order.

2. Facilitate the process of getting acquainted

3. Facilitate the process of setting goals.

4. Moderate disagreements or discussions.

5. Acknowledge and respond to learners' feelings.

6. Bring discussion to satisfactory ending by restating, summarizing, and clarifying positions.

7. Adjourn a particular session.

8. Disband the one-to-one pair or small group when the time comes.

Note that 4, 5, and 6 above are roles from which you will increasingly withdraw and in which students will increasingly take more active roles.

Instructor. In addition to being the housekeeper and the facilitator, you also have the role of instructor. You will decide on the support materials, continue to help clarify objectives during the sessions, and develop lesson plans as your assessment of learners' progress evolves.

If you notice a group member who would really benefit from additional one-to-one instruction, you might want to intervene. Ask this learner if he or she would like a personal tutor. In some family literacy programs, for example, four-to-six parents might participate in a group, but two could also have one-to-one tutoring in addition to the group instruction.

As time progresses, you will probably note that the students will begin to be more productive, to show more responsibility for their learning, and to become more accepting of differences. As these things happen, your role as the authority figure will lessen. You set the tone of flexibility and relaxed acceptance.

RESPONSIBILITIES

The tutor's responsibilities are these:

Model. The tutor models an informal "greeting" at the beginning of each session; models the reading of words, lists, sentences, or paragraphs produced by the students; models reading from print material; models giving appropriate comments and asking open-ended questions on the writing pieces.

Set the Tasks. The tutor prepares a clearly defined, clearly achievable task for each session. Much of the instruction for the session will be directly related to this task. These tasks arise out of the individual (and group) goals of the learners.

Ask Questions. Remember to ask instead of tell. Asking questions takes practice for most of us. Traditionally, we supply information instead of eliciting it. Helping learners come up with their own answers through questioning is one of the most valuable tutoring techniques we can learn. Chapter Three lists a variety of useful and reliable questioning strategies.

Commit to Tutoring. A volunteer tutor must make a real commitment to the job. You have the potential to greatly influence at least one person's life by your efforts, so you should agree to do the following:

1. Master tutoring techniques through appropriate training.

2. Continue your training by participating in in-service programs provided by your local literacy program.

3. Teach at least one student at least two hours a week for a minimum of fifty hours a year.

4. Keep records of each student's progress, discussing them with each student as well as with your program coordinator. You might set aside ten or fifteen minutes every month to review each learner's portfolio. Review accomplishments together. In a small group setting, you might do this while the others are working independently on their writing.

5. Plan lessons based on your sense, or assessment, of each student's interests, strengths, and needs. Have appropriate materials available.

6. Report your students' goal achievements, improvement in reading and writing, interest changes, hours of instruction, and changes in self-esteem on the forms supplied to you.

The learners' responsibilities are these:

Make a Specific Time Commitment. It's important that students make a commitment for a definite period of time. This allows students to plan and arrange their schedules, taking additional classes as the need arises. Encourage your students to commit to learning as a lifelong activity.

Participate Actively. Real learning requires active participation. In general, you can expect learners to gradually assume responsibility for some of their own learning. They should:

1. Attend sessions regularly and on time.

2. Call the tutor if unable to attend a session.

3. Participate in making ground rules (no smoking, listen to others, etc.).

4. Help plan individual (and group) goals.

5. Help design activities or strategies to achieve identified goals.

6. Participate in those activities, making positive comments on their own (and others') work and asking clarifying questions.

7. Show respect for each other's rights and opinions.

8. Agree to confidentiality.

9. Do agreed upon homework assignments.

Work Within an Agreement. "How long should I work with my new learner?" "I think that my learner should move to a new learning experience, but how shall I tell him?" "How can I get my student to do homework?" These are questions that might arise.

One way to address these issues is to propose an agreement with students that would be in effect for a specific period of time and be subject to renewal if the circumstances so warrant.

Perhaps you will discover that a student has serious problems and that learning to read and write will necessitate professional help. When the contract period has passed, a new contract might be drawn up giving very specific and limited goals. You might say to your student: "During the next four weeks, I think you can learn forty important words. When you learn these new words, you will be much better off than you were before, and then we'll decide if we should continue lessons." Write up the agreement. In this way you can teach some survival skills and begin to prepare for termination.

Suppose a student has been delinquent in attending lessons. You both review the agreement at the end of the designated period, and you can say very frankly, "Well, there were a good many times you missed your lesson. I think you've got so many other things you're concerned about that learning to read and write better isn't the highest thing on your list right now. Perhaps later on you'll be ready for more lessons."

When you, as a tutor, are certain that your student has truly tried, but is just not learning, be honest about it. You might say, "You know, reading is really tough and all of us are not made the same. There's lots about reading that we just don't know. Let's go to the program coordinator to see if we can find you some more help." This makes it possible for both learner and tutor to break off their relationship with some measure of dignity.

The agreement system might well provide an "out" for the learner who isn't learning but who hesitates to make the break. If the contract expires within a specific time, there is no danger of either the learner or the tutor being trapped in a fruitless situation.

On the other hand, if the learner has made progress, you can say at the end of the agreement period, "Look at all you've learned. Now that you know how to learn, you can learn even more. So, let's discuss our agreement for the next ten weeks."

A sample Learner/Tutor Agreement form is in the Appendix on page 181. Give a signed copy to your student and keep one for yourself.

Do Homework Assignments. A major part of each student's responsibility is to agree to some home practice. Discuss and plan with the tutor the amount of time and the kind of homework activities that are appropriate.

PLAN SCHEDULE AND CONFIRM SITE

After you have introduced each other, encouraged participation, and discussed roles and responsibilities together, then you can plan the schedule, confirm the site, and review goals and interests.

One of the first decisions the learning partnership will make concerns the frequency and duration of the sessions. Make certain that time and meeting site are confirmed.

It may very well be that the location of the sessions will have a significant influence on the frequency and duration of the sessions. Accessibility, availability of public transportation, expense, and ride-sharing possibilities are all elements to be considered in choosing an acceptable site.

There are no hard and fast rules, but one-to-one teams usually meet twice a week for at least an hour per session. Experience has shown that for small groups, two sessions per week, each of two hours' duration, is an effective pattern.

After several weeks of following the initial schedule, together you can evaluate the schedule's appropriateness. You can always change the schedule.

REVIEW GOALS AND COMPLETE LESSON

You will be assessing your students' performance levels in reading and writing, as well as their self-confidence, as your lessons progress. Noting where your students start gives you a base line for showing improvement.

You are responsible for following or adapting your daily lesson plan and for completing each lesson. It could include any of the reading and writing strategies you have learned as well as games and reinforcing strategies.

WRAP UP

Then go to the wrap up portion of the lesson. Do not forget to evaluate with your students what each liked about the session, then decide on the home practice assignment. Remind them of the ground rules you set together as to attendance, punctuality, and notifying each other if tutoring appointments cannot be kept.

End the session reading an inspiring or humorous selection to your students. Some tutors have found that a "continued next session" mystery keeps the students coming back for more.

HOME PRACTICE

Remind the students of their homework assignments, making sure they completely understand what you have agreed on for them to do. Don't forget to include your own homework assignments: review, record, plan, get required materials. Now you're ready for the next lesson.

With students and tutor accepting their roles and responsibilities, lessons should proceed smoothly. Be ready to adapt and change if circumstances warrant. Working as a team, you can surely predict success.

Planning the First Lesson

Preparation

1. Review student information.

2. Select material.

3. Contact learners, set time and place for meeting.

The Tutoring Lesson

1. Introduce each other.

2. Encourage participation.

3. Discuss rules, responsibilities, and roles.

4. Plan schedule and confirm site.

5. Review goals and interest information as you work together.

6. Teach.

7. Wrap up.

8. Home practice, review of notes.

SUMMARY

Once tutors and students are matched and meet together, the learning and sharing begin. Well planned lessons form the basis for success, but tutors must be willing to adapt their best laid plans to students' often changing needs. Plan ahead, but be prepared to change and adapt. Exciting and challenging days are ahead for both tutors and students.

◆◆◆

EPILOGUE

◆ **ONE-TO-ONE**

◆ **SMALL GROUP**

◆ **MAKING A DIFFERENCE**

ON DOWN THE ROAD

AS YOU HAVE READ THIS BOOK, you have gained many skills. These skills should enable you to be successful with your very first student. However, it is only as you use your skills again and again that you will become really proficient as a reading and writing tutor. As you work, you will create, adapt, and find new ways to help your students. We encourage you to take advantage of continued in-service training. Whether you teach one-to-one or in a small group, let's look at what you can expect within a short time of tutoring.

ONE-TO-ONE

After a few months together in one-to-one sessions, most tutors and students have become friends. They've found things of mutual interest and concern and feel free to discuss personal and even controversial subjects. Even their greetings are personal: "How is Bobby feeling?" Or a student can't wait to tell his tutor good news: "You'll never guess—I got a promotion at work" or "I got a reply from that letter I wrote asking for information on bus travel."

Although the tutor has a lesson plan, students know that they can ask for immediate help in whatever area they indicate. One day they may work on a job application; another on a note to a child's teacher; and yet another on reading and discussing an article on the local baseball team.

SMALL GROUP

If you were to walk into a collaborative small group session after they had been working together for a few weeks, you might be greeted by the following scene. Two learners are discussing their papers with each other, reading parts aloud, asking questions, listening, and providing feedback. In another part of the room, a learner is listening to a tape and writing at the same time. The tutor and a fourth learner are spending some time working with capitalization. After a few minutes, the tutor joins the person with the tape recorder and then is called to join the two learners discussing their papers.

Doesn't look like group work, does it? But you have walked in on this group at a time during their two-hour session when learners have been through a group sequence and are now doing those things they can do alone, with a tutor or with a peer. Other parts of the lesson will involve the whole group.

MAKING A DIFFERENCE

I am only one,
But still I am one.
I cannot do everything,
But still I can do something;
And because I cannot do everything
I will not refuse to do the something
    that I can do.

Edward Everett Hale

Whether you teach one-to-one or in a small group, your life will change, and you will have touched the life of at least one other person. But in reality you may have influenced many lives—students' children, families, friends, co-workers. Who knows how far the ripple effects may go?

As you are out there, sometimes feeling alone and insignificant, as you contemplate the overwhelming task of teaching millions to read and write, remember that there are thousands of tutors, sitting as you are, teaching one-to-one, teaching a small group. You are indeed opening new doors; you are breaking down barriers—cultural, economic, educational, racial. Good luck and know that together we will make a difference.

♦♦♦

APPENDIX

◆ APPENDIX

APPENDIX

◆ **PROLITERACY WORLDWIDE FACT SHEET**

◆ **LEARNER GOALS AND INTERESTS**

◆ **READING/WRITING INVENTORY**

◆ **LISTENING SKILLS**

◆ **D'NEALIAN™ ALPHABET**

◆ **PERSONAL WORD LIST**

◆ **THREE HUNDRED MOST FREQUENTLY USED WORDS IN RANK ORDER**

◆ **SIGNS IN CAPITALS**

◆ **USEFUL WORDS FOR FILLING OUT FORMS**

◆ **SUGGESTED KEY WORDS**

◆ **WORD PATTERNS**

◆ **LEARNER/TUTOR AGREEMENT**

◆ **DISCOVERY METHOD FOR SKILLS AND DRILLS**

◆ **SPELLING AND THE ADULT STUDENT**

◆ **TEACHING SUGGESTIONS FOR ADULTS WITH SUSPECTED LEARNING DISABILITIES/ DIFFERENCES**

◆ **CHECKLIST FOR THE EVALUATION OF ADULT BASIC READING MATERIAL**

◆ **LESSON PLAN**

◆ **LESSON PLAN (ALTERNATE FORM)**

◆ **BIBLIOGRAPHY**

◆ **TO ORDER MATERIALS**

APPENDIX

THIS APPENDIX REPRESENTS MATERIALS to supplement the major areas covered in this handbook. It is arranged in the general order of the text for ease in reference. The word lists are provided for the convenient reference of the tutors. However, as explained in the text, collaborative tutoring takes place within student-centered contexts. Most of the materials included were created or adapted by ProLiteracy America and its affiliate network. Additional handouts are provided during the training.

New insights may be gained when exploring the Bibliography. A catalog describing the materials and services available from New Readers Press will be sent upon request (see page 197). It includes core training materials in Basic Literacy, English as a Second Language, and Program Management, as well as support publications. Contact ProLiteracy Worldwide or other national literacy providers for additional resources and information.

PROLITERACY WORLDWIDE FACT SHEET

PROLITERACY WORLDWIDE is a nonprofit, 501(c)(3) educational corporation. Its mission is to sponsor educational programs and services designed to empower adults and their families by assisting them to acquire the literacy practices and skills they need to function more effectively in their daily lives and participate in the transformation of their societies. ProLiteracy Worldwide provides these programs and services through:

- **ProLiteracy America** (the U.S. Programs Division)
- **New Readers Press** (the U.S. Publishing Division)
- **The International Programs Division**

ProLiteracy America is the U.S. Programs Division of ProLiteracy Worldwide. Its purpose is to advocate for the needs of adult learners and to provide support to the organizations and agencies that serve them. Examples of this support include the following:

- technical assistance and training
- an annual conference with a broad range of training opportunities
- an accreditation system for local literacy programs
- a certification system for trainers who conduct staff development workshops for instructors

New Readers Press (NRP), the U.S. Publishing Division of ProLiteracy Worldwide, is an award-winning publisher that works with authors, educators, and top-name consultants to develop instructional materials and resources for instructors and volunteer tutors. One of NRP's most widely-read publications is its weekly newspaper for adult new readers: *News For You.*

The International Programs Division works with 82 international partner organizations that provide literacy programs in 47 developing countries in Asia, Africa, Latin America, and the Middle East. ProLiteracy's "Literacy Solutions" process allows learners to develop native-language literacy skills while at the same time acquiring information they need to solve problems unique to their communities (nutrition, health, safe drinking water, transportation, employment, etc.)

In addition, ProLiteracy Worldwide has two major grant programs:

- **Women in Literacy [www.womeninliteracy.org]:** Women in Literacy expands literacy instruction to include application projects such as cooperatives, healthcare programs, small business opportunities, and human rights campaigns designed to address the concerns of women and their communities.
- **National Book Scholarship Fund [www.nbsf.org]:** Since 1995, donors have made possible the distribution of $1.5 million worth of books and literacy materials to 730 literacy projects.

ProLiteracy Worldwide receives little government funding, relying instead on revenue from its publishing division and on the generous support of individuals, foundations, corporations, and community groups.

Contributions to ProLiteracy Worldwide are tax deductible to the extent allowed by law.

CONTACTS

ProLiteracy Worldwide or ProLiteracy America
1320 Jamesville Avenue
Syracuse, New York 13210
(315) 422-9121
info@proliteracy.org; www.proliteracy.org

New Readers Press
P.O. Box 35888
Syracuse, New York 13235-5888
(800) 448-8878
www.newreaderspress.org

◆◆◆

ProLiteracy Worldwide was created in 2002 through the merger of Laubach Literacy International and Literacy Volunteers of America, Inc.

LEARNER GOALS AND INTERESTS

TO THE TUTOR/INTERVIEWER: You need to know why learners are in the program, and what their expectations and interests are as you work together to plan lessons.

Directions: During an informal discussion ask the learners why they are in the program and what they might like to do once they can read and write better. Do not read this list to the learners. Record each learner's stated goals or check off topics as mentioned. After the session transfer the information to the intake form. This Goals and Interests summary becomes part of the learner's portfolio.

LEARNER'S STATED GOALS

_____

_____

_____

_____

_____

_____

_____

COMMUNITY (1)
❏ Apply for Citizenship
❏ Participate in Neighborhood Watch
❏ Read for Community Activities
❏ Read/Write for Newsletter
❏ Read for Religious Activities (Bible, Talmud, etc.)

DRIVER'S LICENSE (2)
❏ Apply for Driver's License
❏ Take Driver's Test
❏ Receive License

GED (3)
❏ Register for GED Classes
❏ Complete GED

JOB/BETTER JOB (4)
❏ Read Classified Ads
❏ Fill Out Applications
❏ Apply for Armed Services
❏ Take Test for a Job
❏ Read Notes from Co-Workers
❏ Write Notes to Co-Workers
❏ Read Work-Related Materials
❏ Write Reports
❏ Read Manuals
❏ Fill Out Orders/Requisitions
❏ Read Equipment Operating Instructions

SURVIVAL SKILLS (5)
❑ Read Menus
❑ Read Recipes
❑ Write Shopping Lists
❑ Read Cooking Directions/Food Labels
❑ Read Newspapers/Magazines
❑ Read Bills
❑ Write Checks
❑ Balance Checkbook to Statement
❑ Open/Use Checking/Savings Accounts
❑ Apply for Safety Deposit Box
❑ Apply for Unemployment Insurance
❑ Complete Credit/Loan Application
❑ Read Lease/Rental Agreement
❑ Read Medication Labels/Prescriptions
❑ Read Labels in Drug Store
❑ Apply for Medicare/Medicaid/HMO
❑ Fill Out Insurance Forms
❑ Read Bus/Airline/Train Schedules
❑ Read Travel Guides/Maps
❑ Read Car Repair Invoices
❑ Read Info in Phone Book/Find Number/
   Address/Yellow Pages

PARENTING SKILLS (6)
❑ Read Notes from School
❑ Write Notes to School
❑ Read to Child
❑ Help Child with Homework
❑ Read/Write Cards/Letters
❑ Participate in PTA/PTO
❑ Participate in Scouting Program

VOTING (7)
❑ Register to Vote
❑ Read Ballot and Vote

OTHER EDUCATION/TRAINING (8)
❑ Enter Training Program
❑ Take Adult Basic Education (ABE) Classes
❑ Enter Adult Basic Education (ABE) Program
❑ Apply for College

LIBRARY/CREATIVE (9)
❑ Apply for Library Card
❑ Read in Library
❑ Check Out Books
❑ Check Out A/V Materials
❑ Use Reference Materials
❑ Write Journal, Stories, Poems, Essays

Date _____

Learner's Name _____

Interviewer _____

READING/WRITING INVENTORY

AS THE TUTOR/INTERVIEWER, you might say: "This list of questions is about what you do read or write or what you might like to read or write. We'll be talking about newspapers, books, magazines, and other materials like letters, advertisements, school notices, and signs."

Date _____

Learner's Name _____

Interviewer _____

A. General: "Do you usually read any of the following?" If "yes," ask how often? (*Read this list to the learner.*)

KIND	DAILY	WEEKLY	SEVERAL TIMES A MONTH
Business Letters			
Personal Letters			
School Notices			
Ads			
Grocery Lists			
Menus			
Television Guides			
Job Directions			
Application Blanks/Forms			
Books to Children			
Junk Mail			
Other			

B. Newspapers: "Have you looked at any newspapers in the last six months?" If "no," go to C. If "yes," ask "What part of the paper? How often do you read it?" (*Do **not** read this list to the learner.*)

PART	DAILY	WEEKLY	SEVERAL TIMES A MONTH
Front Page			
Local News			
Sports Page			
Ads			
Comics			
Obits/Society			
Ann Landers/Dear Abby			
Horoscopes			
Letters to the Editor			
Other			

C. Books: "Have you looked through any books in the last six months?" If "no," go to D. If "yes," ask "What kinds of books? How often do you read them?" (*Do **not** read this list to the learner.*)

KIND	DAILY	WEEKLY	SEVERAL TIMES A MONTH
Manuals			
Mysteries			
Romances			
Sports			
Cook Books			
Gardening			
Religious			
Other			

D. Magazines: "Have you looked at any magazines in the last six months?" If "no," go to E. If "yes," ask "What kinds of magazines? How often do you read them?" (*Do **not** read this list to the learner.*)

KIND	DAILY	WEEKLY	SEVERAL TIMES A MONTH
How to Fix It			
Romances			
Sports			
Gardening			
Women's			
Fashion			
Hunting/Fishing			
News			
Other			

E. Reading Materials for Lessons: "Of the kinds of reading materials that we just talked about, are there any you would like to use in our lessons? Which ones?" (*Circle the ones the learner mentions.*)

F. Writing: "Do you usually write any of the following?" If "yes," ask how often? (*Read this list to the learner.*)

KIND	DAILY	WEEKLY	SEVERAL TIMES A MONTH
Grocery Lists			
Business Letters			
Notes at Work			
Personal Notes			
Notes to School			
Letters/Cards			
Journal/Diary			
Catalog Orders			
Work Reports			
Checks			
Other			

LISTENING SKILLS

AT THE BEGINNING of each lesson, take time to talk with your students to find out their feelings and opinions about the lessons and what is happening in their lives. This time is well spent and will reap the benefits of increased learning.

Practicing listening skills will be the basis of communication with your students. You can use these skills in your lessons to keep the focus on your students and their concerns. Here are some important listening skills that you should know and use.

A. REFLECTIVE LISTENING: Responding to a person by giving back both the message and the feelings in a tentative manner.

♦ *Parroting:* Repeating exactly, word for word, what the other person has said.

♦ *Paraphrasing:* Giving back the speaker's idea in your own words, rather than repeating the speaker's words.

♦ *Focus Questioning:* Helping the speaker keep to the point he/she is making, asking questions like: "Just what is it that you don't understand?" "What did you like about today's lesson?"

B. ENCOURAGING SKILLS: Letting the speaker know he/she is being heard.

♦ *Interested Silence:* Helping the speaker talk about a difficult problem, because you give him/her space to think before you react.

♦ *Door Openers:* Issuing an invitation to the other to speak through cues—silence, or words that indicate you are willing and have the time to listen. Use phrases such as: "You seem troubled." "You sure look excited." "How did it go?"

♦ *Open-Ended Questions:* Encouraging the speaker to elaborate by bringing ideas to mind that the person isn't aware of. For example, ask "What do you want to do now?" rather than suggesting a course of action.

C. SUMMARIZING: Stating the main points of the other's conversation in two or three sentences.

D'NEALIAN™ ALPHABET

D'NEALIAN™ MANUSCRIPT ALPHABET

a b c d e f g h i j k l m

n o p q r s t u v w x y z

A B C D E F G H I J K L M

N O P Q R S T U V W X Y Z

D'NEALIAN™ CURSIVE ALPHABET

a b c d e f g h i j k l m

n o p q r s t u v w x y z

A B C D E F G H I

J K L M N O P 2

R S T U V W X Y Z

D'NEALIAN™ NUMBERS

0 1 2 3 4 5 6 7 8 9

PERSONAL WORD LIST

Name

THREE HUNDRED MOST FREQUENTLY USED WORDS IN RANK ORDER

the	has	also	day	high	going	need
of	when	did	same	upon	look	four
and	who	many	another	school	asked	within
to	will	before	know	every	later	felt
a	more	must	while	don't	knew	along
in	no	through	last	does	point	children
that	if	back	might	got	next	saw
is	out	years	us	united	program	best
was	so	where	great	left	city	church
he	said	much	old	number	business	ever
for	what	your	year	course	give	least
it	up	way	off	war	group	power
with	its	well	come	until	toward	development
as	about	down	since	always	young	light
his	into	should	against	away	days	thing
on	than	because	go	something	let	seemed
be	them	each	came	fact	room	family
at	can	just	right	though	president	interest
by	only	those	used	water	side	want
I	other	people	take	less	social	members
this	new	Mr.	three	public	given	mind
had	some	how	states	put	present	country
not	could	too	himself	think	several	area
are	time	little	few	almost	order	others
but	these	state	house	hand	national	done
from	two	good	use	enough	possible	turned
or	may	very	during	far	rather	although
have	then	make	without	took	second	open
an	do	world	again	head	face	God
they	first	still	place	yet	per	service
which	any	own	American	government	among	certain
one	my	see	around	system	form	kind
you	now	men	however	better	important	problem
were	such	work	home	set	often	began
her	like	long	small	told	things	different
all	our	get	found	nothing	looked	door
she	over	here	Mrs.	night	early	thus
there	man	between	thought	end	white	help
would	me	both	went	why	case	sense
their	even	life	say	called	John	means
we	most	being	part	didn't	become	whole
him	made	under	once	eyes	large	matter
been	after	never	general	find	big	

Henry Kucera and W. Nelson Francis, *Computational Analysis of Present-Day American English* (Providence: Brown University Press, 1967).

SIGNS IN CAPITALS

A minimum list of words and phrases one should be able to read for physical safety, social acceptability, and avoidance of embarrassment.

GENERAL SIGNS

ADULTS ONLY

ANTIDOTE

BEWARE

BEWARE OF THE DOG

BUS STATION

BUS STOP

CAUTION

CLOSED

COMBUSTIBLE

CONTAMINATED

COMDEMNED

DANGER

DEEP WATER

DENTIST

DON'T WALK

DO NOT CROSS, USE TUNNEL

DO NOT CROWD

DO NOT ENTER

DO NOT INHALE FUMES

DO NOT PUSH

DO NOT REFREEZE

DO NOT SHOVE

DO NOT STAND UP

DO NOT USE NEAR HEAT

DO NOT USE NEAR OPEN FLAME

DOCTOR (DR.)

DOWN

DYNAMITE

ELEVATOR

EMERGENCY EXIT

EMPLOYEES ONLY

ENTRANCE

EXIT

EXPLOSIVES

EXTERNAL USE ONLY

FALLOUT SHELTER

FIRE ESCAPE

FIRE EXTINGUISHER

FIRST AID

FLAMMABLE

FOUND

FRAGILE

GASOLINE

GATE

GENTLEMEN

HANDLE WITH CARE

HANDS OFF

HELP

HIGH VOLTAGE

IN

INFLAMMABLE

INFORMATION

INSTRUCTIONS

KEEP AWAY

KEEP CLOSED AT ALL TIMES

KEEP OFF (THE GRASS)

KEEP OUT

LADIES

LOST

LIVE WIRES

MEN

NEXT (WINDOW GATE)

NO ADMITTANCE

NO CHECKS CASHED

NO CREDIT

NO DIVING

NO DOGS ALLOWED

NO DUMPING

NO FIRES

NO LOITERING

NO FISHING

NO HUNTING

NO MINORS

NO SMOKING

NO SPITTING

NO SWIMMING

NO TOUCHING

NO TRESPASSING

NOT FOR INTERNAL USE

NOXIOUS

NURSE

OFFICE

OPEN

OUT

OUT OF ORDER

PEDESTRIANS

PROHIBITED

POISON

POISONOUS

POLICE (STATION)

POST NO BILLS

POST OFFICE

POSTED

PRIVATE

PRIVATE PROPERTY

PULL

PUSH

SAFETY FIRST

SHALLOW WATER

SHELTER

SMOKING PROHIBITED

STEP DOWN (UP)

TAXI STAND

TERMS CASH

THIN ICE

THIS END UP

THIS SIDE UP

UP

USE IN OPEN AIR

USE OTHER DOOR

USE BEFORE (DATE)

VIOLATORS WILL BE PROSECUTED

WALK

WANTED

WARNING

WATCH YOUR STEP

WET PAINT

WOMEN

CAR RELATED SIGNS

ALL CARS (TRUCKS) STOP

ASK ATTENDANT FOR KEY

BEWARE OF CROSS WINDS

BRIDGE OUT

BUS ONLY

CAUTION

CONSTRUCTION ZONE

CURVE

DANGEROUS CURVE

DEAD END

DEER (CATTLE) CROSSING

DETOUR

DIM LIGHTS

DIP

DO NOT BLOCK WALK (DRIVEWAY)

DO NOT ENTER

DRIFTING SAND

DRIVE SLOW

EMERGENCY VEHICLES ONLY

END 45

END CONSTRUCTION

ENTRANCE

EXIT ONLY

EXIT SPEED 30

FALLING ROCKS

FLOODED

FLOODS WHEN RAINING

FOUR WAY STOP

FREEWAY

GARAGE

GATE

GO SLOW

HOSPITAL ZONE

INSPECTION STATION

JUNCTION 101A

KEEP TO THE LEFT (RIGHT)

LANE ENDS

LAST CHANCE FOR GAS

LEFT LANE MUST TURN LEFT

LEFT TURN ON THIS SIGNAL ONLY

LEFT TURN ONLY

LEFT TURN O.K.

LOADING ZONE

LOOK

LOOK OUT FOR CARS (TRUCKS)

LISTEN

M.P.H.

MECHANIC ON DUTY

MEN WORKING

MERGE LEFT (RIGHT)

MERGING TRAFFIC

MILITARY RESERVATION

NEXT

NO PARKING

NO LEFT TURN

NO PASSING

NO RIGHT TURN

NO RIGHT TURN ON RED LIGHT

NO SMOKING AREA

NO STANDING

NO STOPPING

NO TURNS

NO "U" TURN

NOT A THROUGH STREET

ONE WAY DO NOT ENTER

ONE WAY STREET

PAVEMENT ENDS

PLAYGROUND

PROCEED AT YOUR OWN RISK

PRIVATE ROAD

PUT ON CHAINS

R.R.

RAILROAD CROSSING

REST ROOMS

RESUME SPEED

RIGHT LANE MUST TURN RIGHT

RIGHT TURN ONLY

ROAD CLOSED

ROAD ENDS

SCHOOL STOP

SCHOOL ZONE

SLIDE AREA

SLIPPERY WHEN WET (FROSTY)

SLOW DOWN

SLOWER TRAFFIC KEEP RIGHT

SPEED CHECKED BY RADAR

STEEP GRADE

STOP

STOP FOR PEDESTRIANS

STOP WHEN OCCUPIED

STOP MOTOR

THIS LANE MAY TURN LEFT

THIS ROAD PATROLLED BY

AIRCRAFT

THREE WAY LIGHT

TURN OFF

TURN OFF 1\2 MILE (1/4 MILE)

TRAFFIC CIRCLE

TRUCK ROUTE

UNLOADING ZONE

USE LOW GEAR

WATCH FOR FLAGMAN

WATCH FOR LOW FLYING AIRCRAFT

WINDING ROAD

YIELD

YIELD RIGHT OF WAY

USEFUL WORDS FOR FILLING OUT FORMS

date	zip code	divorced	weekly
month	city	widowed	part-time
year	state	single	full-time
name	telephone number	occupation	temporary work
Mr.	business telephone	employer	sex
Mrs.	home telephone	firm	male
Miss	citizen	place of employment	female
Ms.	citizenship status	self-employed	health plan coverage
first name	birthdate	length of service	medical history
last name	date of birth	references	physical impairment
maiden name	place of birth	in case of emergency	driver's license number
middle name	age	education	signature
middle initial	height	years of schooling	residence
address	weight	last school attended	insurance
street	Social Security number	degrees held	dependents
permanent address	marital status	diplomas held	
mailing address	married	salary	
present address	separated	hourly	

SUGGESTED KEY WORDS
When Teaching Initial Consonant Sounds

As you use phonics, keep these three items in mind:

1. Teach only the letter-sound relationships each individual student needs—those identified in the student's assessment.

2. Suggest as possible key words those students can best relate to. Ask the students to pick the key word.

3. Remember that English is not a phonetically regular language. Some consonants have more than one sound or may behave irregularly. For example, the letter *c* has the /*k*/ sound (e.g., *corn, camera*) but it also has the /*s*/ sound (e.g., *ceiling, city*). Also, the letter *k* has no sound in *knife, know*, etc.

B	bus, baby, ball, bed, banana, bag, bird	**C**	cat, cup, can, cake, comb, coffee,
D	dog, dish, doll, desk, doughnut	**C**	cigar, city, cent, celery
F	fish, fan, fire, feet, feather	**G**	gas, girl, game, gate, garage
H	hand, hat, house, ham, horn, hi-fi	**G**	gem, gentleman, giraffe
J	jar, jacket, jet, jug, jeep		***Digraphs***
K	key, kite, king, kerchief	**CH**	church, chair, children
L	leg, lamp, lock, leaf, ladder, leather	**CH**	cholesterol, chemical, choir
M	man, match, money, milk, mother	**CH**	chute, chauffer
N	name, nose, nail, needle	**PH**	phone, photo, pharmacy
P	pot, pan, pig, pants, pipe, pumpkin, pen	**SH**	shoe, ship, shower, shovel
Q (QU)	quarter, queen, quilt, quick	**TH**	this, the, them, these
R	rat, radio, rocket, rope, river, red	**TH**	thumb, thank, theater
S	sun, sink, socks, sandwich	**WH**	wheel, whale, white
T	telephone, towel, table, tub, turkey, tea		
V	valentine, valley, violin, vacuum, van		
W	window, wing, wig, watch, wagon, water		
X*	wax, fix, box, tux		
y	yellow, yarn, yo-yo, yardstick		
z	zipper, zebra, zoo		

*There are no words in English that begin with *x* as it makes the /*ks*/ sound.

WORD PATTERNS

SHORT A SOUNDS

-ab	-ack	-ad	-ag	-am	-amp	-an	-and	-ang	-ank
cab	back	ad	bag	am	camp	an	and	bang	bank
dab	hack	bad	gag	ham	damp	ban	band	fang	rank
gab	jack	cad	hag	jam	lamp	can	hand	gang	sank
jab	pack	dad	lag	clam	champ	fan	land	hang	tank
lab	rack	fad	nag	slam	clamp	man	sand	rang	yank
nab	sack	had	rag	swam	cramp	pan	gland	sang	blank
tab	tack	lad	sag		stamp	ran	grand	tang	clank
blab	black	mad	tag		tramp	tan	stand	clang	plank
flab	slack	pad	wag			van		slang	crank
slab	crack	sad	brag			clan			drank
crab	track	clad	drag			plan			frank
drab	shack	glad	flag			scan			spank
grab	whack	shad	shag			span			thank
scab	smack		snag			than			
stab	snack		stag						
	stack								

-ap	-ash	-asp	-ass	-ast	-at	-atch	-ath	-ax
cap	ash	asp	ass	cast	at	catch	bath	ax
gap	bash	gasp	bass	fast	bat	hatch	path	wax
lap	cash	hasp	lass	last	cat	latch	wrath	flax
map	dash	rasp	mass	mast	fat	match		
nap	gash	clasp	pass	past	hat	patch		
rap	hash		brass	vast	mat	thatch		
sap	lash		grass	blast	pat			
tap	mash		class		rat			
chap	rash		glass		sat			
clap	sash				vat			
flap	clash				brat			
slap	crash				chat			
snap	smash				flat			
trap	stash				slat			
	trash				scat			
					that			

WORD PATTERNS—*continued*

SHORT E SOUNDS

-eck	**-ed**	**-eg**	**-elf**	**-ell**	**-elp**	**-elt**	**-em**	**-en**	**-end**
deck	bed	beg	elf	bell	help	belt	hem	den	end
heck	fed	egg	self	dell	yelp	felt	them	hen	bend
neck	led	keg	shelf	fell		melt	stem	men	lend
peck	red	leg		hell				pen	mend
check	wed	peg		sell				ten	send
speck	bled			tell				glen	blend
	fled			well				then	spend
	sled			yell				when	trend
	shed			quell					
	sped			shell					
				smell					
				spell					
				swell					

-ent	**-ept**	**-ess**	**-est**	**-et**
bent	kept	less	best	bet
dent	wept	mess	nest	get
lent		bless	pest	jet
rent		chess	rest	let
sent		dress	test	met
tent			vest	net
went			west	pet
spent			chest	set
			crest	wet
			quest	yet
				fret

WORD PATTERNS—*continued*

SHORT I SOUNDS

-ib	-ick	-id	-ift	-ig	-ilk	-ill	-im	-in	-inch
bib	kick	bid	gift	big	bilk	bill	dim	in	inch
fib	lick	did	lift	dig	milk	fill	him	bin	cinch
rib	nick	hid	rift	fig	silk	gill	rim	din	pinch
crib	pick	kid	sift	jig		hill	skim	fin	clinch
	sick	lid	drift	pig		kill	slim	kin	
	tick	rid	shift	rig		mill	swim	pin	
	wick	grid	swift	wig		pill	trim	sin	
	brick	skid		brig		rill	whim	tin	
	trick	slid		swig		sill		win	
	chick					till		chin	
	thick					will		shin	
	click					chill		thin	
	flick					drill		grin	
	slick					grill		skin	
	quick					quill		spin	
	stick					spill		twin	
						skill			
						still			

-ing	-ink	-int	-ip	-ish	-iss	-ist	-it	-itch	-ive
bing	ink	hint	dip	dish	hiss	fist	it	itch	give
ring	pink	mint	hip	fish	kiss	list	bit	ditch	live
sing	sink	tint	lip	wish	miss	mist	fit	pitch	
wing	wink	flint	nip	swish	bliss	twist	hit	witch	**-ix**
bring	blink		rip				kit	stitch	fix
fling	slink		sip				lit	switch	mix
sling	stink		tip				pit		six
sting	think		zip				sit		twix
swing			yip				wit		
thing			chip				grit		
			ship				mitt		
			whip				quit		
			flip				slit		
			slip				skit		
			grip				spit		
			trip				twit		
			quip						
			skip						
			snip						

WORD PATTERNS—*continued*

SHORT O SOUNDS

-ob	-ock	-od	-og	-oll	-on	-ond	-ong	-ot	-ox
cob	cock	cod	bog	doll	on	bond	bong	cot	ox
fob	dock	God	cog	loll	don	fond	gong	dot	box
gob	hock	hod	dog	moll	non	pond	long	got	fox
job	lock	nod	fog		yon		song	hot	
rob	mock	pod	hog				tong	not	
mob	pock	rod	jog				wrong	pot	
sob	rock	sod	log				strong	rot	
blob	sock	clod	clog					blot	
slob	tock	plod	frog					clot	
snob	clock	shod	smog					plot	
	flock							slot	
	crock							shot	
	frock							spot	
	shock							trot	
	smock								
	stock								

WORD PATTERNS—*continued*

SHORT U SOUNDS

-ub	-uck	-ud	-uff	-ug	-ull	-um	-ump	-un	-unch
cub	buck	bud	buff	bug	cull	bum	bump	bun	bunch
dub	duck	cud	cuff	dug	dull	gum	dump	fun	lunch
hub	luck	mud	huff	hug	gull	hum	hump	gun	punch
nub	muck	stud	muff	jug	hull	mum	jump	nun	brunch
pub	puck	thud	puff	lug	lull	rum	lump	pun	crunch
rub	suck		bluff	mug	mull	sum	pump	run	
sub	tuck		gruff	pug	null	glum	clump	sun	
tub	chuck		stuff	rug	skull	slum	plump	shun	
club	shuck			tug		drum	slump	spun	
grub	cluck			chug		scum	stump	stun	
stub	pluck			thug		chum	thump		
	stuck			plug					
				slug					
				smug					

-ung	-unk	-up	-us	-ush	-usk	-ust	-ut	-uzz
dung	bunk	up	us	gush	dusk	bust	but	buzz
hung	dunk	cup	bus	hush	husk	dust	cut	fuzz
lung	hunk	pup	plus	lush	tusk	just	gut	
rung	junk	sup	thus	mush		lust	hut	
sung	sunk			rush		must	jut	
clung	chunk			blush		rust	nut	
flung	drunk			flush		crust	rut	
stung	flunk			plush			shut	
swung	skunk			slush				
				brush				
				crush				
				shush				

WORD PATTERNS—*continued*

LONG A SOUNDS

-ace	-ade	-age	-aid	-ail	-aim	-ain	-aint	-ait	-ale
ace	fade	age	aid	ail	aim	gain	faint	bait	ale
face	jade	cage	laid	bail	maim	main	paint	gait	dale
lace	lade	page	maid	fail		pain	saint	wait	gale
mace	made	rage	paid	hail		rain	quaint	trait	hale
pace	wade	sage	raid	jail		vain			kale
race	blade	wage	braid	mail		brain			male
brace	glade	stage		nail		drain			pale
place	grade			pail		grain			sale
space	trade			rail		train			tale
	shade			sail		chain			vale
	spade			tail		plain			scale
				vail		slain			shale
				wail		stain			stale
				frail					whale
				quail					
				snail					
				trail					

-ame	-ane	-ape	-ase	-aste	-ate	-ave	-ay	-aze	-eigh
came	cane	ape	base	baste	ate	cave	bay	daze	eight
dame	lane	cape	case	haste	date	gave	day	faze	sleigh
fame	mane	gape	vase	paste	fate	nave	gay	gaze	weigh
game	pane	nape		taste	gate	pave	hay	haze	
lame	sane	rape		waste	hate	rave	jay	maze	
name	vane	tape		chaste	late	save	lay	raze	
same	wane	drape			mate	wave	may	blaze	
tame	crane	grape			rate	brave	nay	glaze	
blame		shape			sate	crave	pay	graze	
flame					crate	grave	ray		
frame					grate	shave	say		
shame					plate	slave	way		
					skate		clay		
					slate		play		
					state		fray		
							gray		
							tray		
							stay		
							sway		

WORD PATTERNS—*continued*

LONG E SOUNDS

-e	-ea	-each	-ead	-eak	-eal	-eam	-ean	-eap	-eat
be	pea	each	bead	beak	deal	beam	bean	heap	eat
he	sea	beach	lead	leak	heal	ream	dean	leap	beat
me	tea	peach	read	peak	meal	seam	lean	reap	feat
we	flea	reach	plead	weak	peal	team	mean	cheap	heat
she	plea	teach		bleak	real	cream	wean		meat
		bleach		freak	seal	dream	clean	**-east**	neat
				speak	veal	gleam	glean	east	peat
					zeal			beast	seat
					steal			feast	cheat
								least	cleat
									pleat
									treat
									wheat

-eech	-eed	-ee	-eef	-eek	-eel	-eem	-eep	-eet	-ief
beech	deed	bee	beef	leek	eel	deem	beep	beet	brief
leech	feed	fee	reef	meek	feel	seem	deep	feet	chief
	heed	see		peek	heel	teem	jeep	meet	grief
	need	tee		reek	keel		keep	fleet	thief
	seed	wee		seek	peel	**-een**	peep	greet	
	weed	free		week	reel	keen	seep	sheet	**-y**
	bleed	tree		cheek		seen	weep	sleet	carry
	breed	glee		creek		teen	creep	sweet	marry
	creed	thee		sleek		green	sheep	tweet	bunny
	freed	three				queen	sleep		funny
	greed					sheen	steep		sunny
	speed						sweep		
	steed								
	tweed								

WORD PATTERNS—*continued*

LONG I SOUNDS

-ice	-ide	-ie	-ife	-igh	-ight	-ike	-ild	-ile	-ime
lice	bide	die	life	high	fight	bike	mild	file	dime
mice	hide	lie	rife	nigh	light	dike	wild	mile	lime
nice	ride	pie	wife	sigh	might	hike	child	pile	time
rice	side	tie		thigh	night	like		rile	chime
vice	tide	vie			right	mike		tile	crime
slice	wide				sight	pike		vile	grime
spice	bride				tight	spike		smile	slime
twice	glide				bright			while	
	slide				fright				
					flight				
					plight				
					slight				

-ind	-ine	-ipe	-ire	-ise	-ite	-ive	-y	-ye
bind	dine	pipe	ire	rise	bite	dive	by	dye
find	fine	ripe	dire	wise	kite	five	my	eye
hind	line	wipe	fire		mite	hive	cry	lye
kind	mine	gripe	hire		site	live	dry	rye
mind	nine	swipe	mire		quite	chive	fly	
rind	pine		sire		spite	drive	ply	
wind	tine		tire		white		fry	
blind	vine		wire				shy	
grind	shine						sky	
	spine						sly	
	swine						spy	
	thine						sty	
	twine						thy	
	whine						try	

WORD PATTERNS—*continued*

LONG O SOUND

-o	-oad	-oam	-oast	-oat	-obe	-ode	-oe	-oke	-old
go	goad	foam	boast	oat	lobe	ode	doe	coke	old
no	load	loam	coast	boat	robe	bode	foe	joke	bold
so	road	roam	roast	coat	globe	code	hoe	poke	cold
	toad		toast	goat		mode	toe	woke	gold
				moat		rode	woe	yoke	hold
				bloat				bloke	mold
				float				choke	sold
				gloat				smoke	told
								spoke	

-oach: coach, poach, roach

-oal: coal, goal

-oan: loan, moan, roan, groan

-ole	-olt	-ome	-one	-ope	-ose	-ost	-ote	-ove	-ow
dole	bolt	dome	bone	cope	hose	host	note	cove	bow
hole	colt	home	cone	dope	nose	most	rote	dove	low
mole	dolt	Nome	lone	hope	pose	post	tote	rove	mow
pole	jolt		pone	mope	rose		vote	wove	row
role	volt		tone	rope	chose		quote		sow
stole			zone	scope	those				tow
			shone	slope	close				blow
			stone						flow
									glow
									slow
									crow
									grow
									show
									snow

LONG U SOUNDS

-ew	-ule	-use	-ute
few	mule	use	cute
hew	yule	fuse	mute
blew		muse	flute
flew			
slew			
chew			
crew			
drew			
grew			
stew			

WORD PATTERNS—*continued*

OTHER SOUNDS IN WORD PATTERNS

-all	-alk	-ar	-arch	-arge	-ark	-arm	-arn	-arp	-arsh
all	talk	bar	march	barge	bark	farm	barn	carp	harsh
ball	walk	car	parch	large	dark	harm	darn	harp	marsh
call	chalk	far	starch	charge	hark	charm	yarn	sharp	
fall	stalk	jar			lark				
gall		par			mark				
hall		tar			park				
mall		scar			shark				
tall		star			spark				
wall					stark				
small									
stall									

-aught	-aul	-aunch	-aunt	-ause	-aw	-awl	-en	-er	-ern
caught	haul	haunch	gaunt	cause	caw	awl	brighten	either	fern
naught	maul	launch	haunt	pause	jaw	bawl	dampen	fatter	stern
taught		paunch	jaunt	clause	law	brawl	darken	matter	
		staunch	taunt		maw	crawl	freshen	poorer	
			vaunt		raw	shawl	hasten	richer	
					saw		lengthen	scatter	
					chaw		shorten		
					claw		silken		
					flaw				
					draw				

-ew	-ird	-irl	-irt	-oard	-oice	-oil	-oin	-oint	-oise
dew	bird	girl	dirt	board	voice	oil	coin	joint	noise
Jew	gird	swirl	shirt	hoard	choice	boil	loin	point	poise
new	third	twirl	skirt			coil			
brew		whirl	squirt			foil			
crew						soil			
drew						toil			
grew						broil			
chew						spoil			
flew									
slew									
stew									

-oist	-oo	-ood	-ook	-ool	-oom	-oon	-oop	-oost	-oot
foist	boo	food	book	cool	boom	boon	coop	boost	boot
hoist	coo	mood	cook	fool	doom	coon	hoop	roost	hoot
joist	moo	brood	hook	pool	loom	goon	loop		loot
moist	too		look	drool	room	loon	droop		root
	zoo		nook	spool	zoom	moon	troop		toot
	shoo		took	stool	gloom	noon	scoop		scoot
			brook		groom	soon	stoop		shoot
			crook			spoon	swoop		
			shook			swoon			

-ooth	-or	-ord	-ore	-ork	-orm	-orn	-ort	-orth	-ouch
booth	or	cord	ore	cork	form	born	fort	forth	ouch
tooth	for	ford	wore	fork	norm	corn	sort	north	couch
	nor	lord	chore	pork	storm	horn	tort		pouch
			score	York		morn			vouch
			swore	stork		torn			
						worn			

-ought	-ould	-ound	-our	-ouse	-out	-outh	-ow	-owl	-own
ought	could	bound	four	house	out	mouth	bow	owl	down
bought	would	found	pour	louse	bout	south	cow	cowl	gown
fought	should	hound		mouse	gout		how	fowl	town
sought		mound			pout		now	howl	brown
brought		pound			shout		vow	jowl	crown
thought		round			spout		wow	yowl	clown
		sound			stout		plow		frown
		wound			trout				
		ground							

-sion	-tion	-ude	-ue	-uke	-ull	-une	-ush	-ute
decision	action	dude	rue	duke	bull	dune	bush	lute
devision	motion	nude	sue	Luke	full	June	push	flute
occasion	nation	rude	blue		pull	tune		
collision	mention	crude	clue					
television	fraction		glue					
	attention		true					

STUDENT/TUTOR AGREEMENT

For a period of _____weeks, from _____to_____

Tutor agrees to:

_____

_____

_____

_____

_____

_____

Student agrees to:

_____

_____

_____

_____

_____

_____

Dated_____   Tutor_____

Student_____

DISCOVERY METHOD FOR SKILLS AND DRILLS

By Judy Cheatham, Ph.D.

Y OU CAN VARY YOUR APPROACH to teaching skills and drills by giving students practice in discovering general rules about our language. This type of teaching is really fun when done in the collaborative group situation.

One example of using the discovery method with students would be to write:

cut	*ceiling*
cat	*cedar*
can	*city*
come	*cider*
cot	*citizen*

Read the first column aloud. Ask the learners to read after you. Then ask, "What beginning sound do you hear in the first list?" Keep asking until you hear /k/. Now say, "What beginning sound do you hear in the second list?" Keep asking until you hear /s/. Now ask, "What's the same about all these words?" "What's different?" You are trying to get learners to say that the letter *c* has two sounds, a /s/ sound and a /k/ sound. Then say, "Figure out what makes one list have the /k/ and the other have the /s/ sound." You are looking for the answer that the *e* or *i* signals an /s/ sound; *o, a, u* signal the /k/.

That's pretty sophisticated stuff! If you taught this (told this) to a group, they would look at you with blank stares, but it's fun and easy if they figure it out for themselves. Phonics or spelling taught this way is definitely not boring— and it's interesting for students to discover these patterns themselves.

For some reason, my learners generally need three tries to state pattern generalizations. Let me give the transcript of my learners formulating a rule for the apostrophe used in forming regular contractions. I wrote the following two lists on the board:

is not	*isn't*
could not	*couldn't*
can not	*can't*
he is	*he's*

I divided the class into small groups of three. Then I said to my class, "Your group has to teach the whole class. The class wants to know how you form a contraction. Talk among yourselves and come up with a rule the class can follow. When you finish, write it on the board."

When it was time to go to the board, all three group members went! They clustered around each other, prodding, giving advice, providing moral support. From almost every group, the rule was, "Two words made into one word by an apostrophe."

So I went to the board, wrote "horse shoe = horse'shoe," and asked, "Is that a contraction?" The response was "No." I asked, "Why not? As you go back to your groups," I continued, "figure out what the difference is between 'is not = isn't' and 'horse shoe = horseshoe.' Look at the lists on the board again and let's take another shot at a rule."

Groups went to the board two more times before their rule fit the examples. The gist of the third try went like this: "Two words made into one by leaving out certain letters that get replaced by the apostrophe, like *can not = can't, is not = isn't.*" I said to the students, "Look on page 87 and somebody read the rule from the book." The students were proud to see that their rule was as accurate as the book's—and very clearly stated!

Of course, many of you will identify the pedagogy used here as inquiry, which is as old as Socrates, or inductive reasoning, which we trace to Sir Francis Bacon. There is nothing new about this type of teaching.

You have excellent resources available to you for developing your own ideas and for supplementing your instruction from New Readers Press. It would be redundant here to repeat all the exercises available. Use spelling, punctuation, and grammar exercises as supplements when a learner needs those kinds of activities. In your diagnosis of a particular learner's writing or reading, you can prescribe certain pages that apply only to him. If you find there are two who need the same work, they can work in pairs in a workshop part of the session. The point is, if only one learner needs help with capitals, for example, don't make the whole small group spend two hours on capitalization.

Any time you work with process activities, you must remember that your goal is for the learner to internalize the generalizations governing the written English language. For that reason, don't tell them; have them tell you. Ask, don't tell. If the group decides a period goes after a group of words, ask why. If the group decides that a word begins with a capital letter, ask why. Accept nothing without trying to get learners to work through and discuss their thought processes and strategies.

Note: A letter in slash marks indicates the letter sound.

SPELLING AND THE ADULT STUDENT

By Lester L. Laminack, Ed.D.

WHAT ABOUT SPELLING? Some people don't want to talk about it because they believe that people can either spell or they can't. Others believe that people can become good spellers by writing lists of words five times each or learning many rules.

What do you think? When you think of "good spellers," what comes to mind? In the space provided jot down three or four characteristics of "good spellers."

A good speller is someone who:

Look at your list above. Would you qualify as a "good speller"? Do you know how to spell all the words you think of when you are writing? Unless you are the rare exception, you probably answered, "Of course not!" Most adults, even those who are very good readers and writers, occasionally have to seek assistance in spelling some words.

What do you do when you are writing and come to a word that you can't spell? In the space below make a list of things you usually do:

Strategies I use to spell words:

Sandra Wilde (1989) has identified these five general strategies that writers use in deciding how to spell words:

1. Placeholder Strategy.

2. Human Resource Strategy.

3. Textual Resource Strategy.

4. Generating, Monitoring, and Revision Strategy.

5. Ownership Strategy.

Do your strategies fall into one or more of these categories?

1. *Placeholder Strategy*. Do you ever write down a few letters and go on, thinking you'll come back and work on the word later? Do you ever write down a letter or two, then draw a line to signal you to return to that word? Do you choose another word that means the same thing?

2. *Human Resource Strategy*. Have you ever been unsure of a word while writing or typing and called out to someone nearby, "Hey how do you spell . . . ?"

3. *Textual Resource Strategy*. When you come across a word you can't spell, do you ever stop to consult a resource like the dictionary, the cover of a book, the return address of an envelope? Do you use the spell checker on a word processor?

4. *Generating, Monitoring, and Revision Strategy*. When you come to a word you are unsure of, do you ever write it one or two different ways to see which one looks right or spell it aloud to check which one sounds right?

5. *Ownership Strategy*. Knowing that you know how to spell a word is ownership. You have ownership over all those words you don't have to think about.

Chances are that you use one or more strategies regularly. Now think about the adult students you will be working with. Many have the perception that good writers spell everything correctly. This totally unrealistic expectation often leaves adult students with a sense of despair and utter inadequacy before they ever begin to write. As a result, many are reluctant to try.

There are some ways you can help, however. Rather than expending tremendous energy on trying to teach dozens of rules and the many exceptions for each, you will find it much less frustrating if you begin helping students monitor their own spellings. Developing the ability to monitor, to determine when you know and when you don't, enables students to begin selecting appropriate strategies for spelling the words they want to use in their writing. The ability to know when a strategy is needed is one you should help them to develop first. Then, students need to be able to select an efficient strategy for spelling the words they choose to write. Your attention should be given to facilitating the students' use of various strategies so as to enable them to become as independent as possible.

As a tutor, you will want to be able to document each student's progress as a speller. The following is a suggested way for keeping track of spelling development and noting patterns in the student's constructive spellings.

Documenting Growth and Development

1. Collect samples of the student's writing over a specified period of time.

2. Count the number of words in each sample.

3. Count the number of different words in each sample. For example, if the word *work* appears in a piece eight times, it will be counted only once.

4. Of the total number of different words, count the number of those spelled conventionally (as in the dictionary).

5. Of the total number of different words, count the number of those words for which the writer constructed/invented a spelling.

6. Divide the number of words spelled conventionally (Step 4) by the total number of different words (Step 3) to determine the "index of control." (See North Carolina First and Second Grade Assessments for Communication Skills, Reading Strategies; State Department of Public Instruction, Raleigh.)

This "index of control" gives you a numerical measure of the writer's control over the spellings of words the writer chooses to use in his or her own writing when given the opportunity to write in his or her own voice.

You may find it helpful to develop a record sheet for documenting the following:

1. Growth in the total number of words used in a writing sample.

2. Growth in the number of different words used in the sample as an indication of increased written verbal fluency.

3. Growth in the writer's "index of control" over spelling.

4. The writer's continuing focus on communication of meaning and sensitivity to word choices.

These can be documented as you see increases in the number of different words accompanied by a steady index of control.

Over time you may notice that the student shows increases in the total number of words, the number of different words, and maintains or increases the "index of control." In this case you would note that the student shows development as a speller in that the total number of words spelled conventionally is increasing. This pattern indicates that the writer is concerned with the expression of ideas and willing to continue taking risks with unknown spellings while gaining control over an increasing number of words used frequently in writing.

If you should notice that the student's writing shows no steady increase in the total number of words and no steady increase in the number of different words paired with an increasing "index of control," your conclusions should be quite different. This scenario could indicate that the writer has shifted the emphasis from expression of ideas and word choice to "using words I can spell." This focus may result in "better" spelling in the individual's written products; however, it may also result in loss of the writer's voice, restricted word choices, and less elaboration on detail. The tutor loses powerful opportunities to note the speller's strategies, strengths, and areas of need.

You may find it helpful to list constructive/invented spellings. Organize them into categories on the basis of similarities in spelling patterns (e.g., -ake, -ight patterns or words where /f/ is spelled ph, etc.). This clustering will be helpful in determining which patterns are most unfamiliar to the writer and to determine where instruction will be most immediately relevant for the student.

Now let's give this a try. Read over the writing sample of a beginning student named Janet. What do you notice immediately?

> I like my tuto Because
> Shee help s'me to ReaD.
> i have learneD aBout the
> Bibele anD new WorDe.
> i RaDeD ni my SuDay
> School
> 　　　　Janet Lee

Chances are that you focused in on the errors that are obvious in the piece. For example, you probably noticed the misplaced capital letters and misspelled words. Your general impression is likely to be less than enthusiastically positive.

Keeping Track of Individual Spelling Growth

A. _____ = # of total words.
B. _____ = # of different words.
C. _____ = # of those spelled conventionally.
D. _____ = # of constructive/invented spellings.

Index of Control = C divided by B.
Index of Control = _____.

Return to the writing sample and make a list of the words used. As you complete the list, note the variety of words used and the spellings.

I i i	to	new
like	ReaD	WorDe (word)
my my	have	RaDeD (read)
tuto (tutor)	learneD	ni (in)
Because	aBout	SuDay (Sunday)
Shee (she)	the	School
help s' (helps)	Bibele (bible)	Janet
me	anD	Lee

A. 27 = # of total words.

B. 24 = # of different words.

C. 16 = # of those spelled conventionally.

D. 08 = # of constructive/invented spellings.

16 divided by 24 = .66 x 100% = 66%.

Index of Control = 66%.

As you first read the passage, did it occur to you that Janet was controlling the spellings for two-thirds of the words she used in her writing? Did you focus on all that Janet could do or was your initial assessment based on collecting evidence regarding her needs? Did you focus on her strengths or her weaknesses?

Let your role be to facilitate students' use of various strategies for spelling unfamiliar words. Record progress by noting increases in written vocabulary (total number of words and number of different words) and in index of control (the percentage of words they can spell conventionally). As you work with adult students, try to focus on what they can do.

TEACHING SUGGESTIONS FOR ADULTS WITH SUSPECTED LEARNING DISABILITIES/DIFFERENCES

By Susan A. Vogel, Ph.D.

SOME ADULTS with severe learning disabilities (LD) or learning differences may need specialized and intensive instruction in order to learn how to read and write; but most will be able to make slow, steady progress. The following are some general teaching suggestions that you can try that are based on principles of learning. They are not unique to the field of learning disabilities. All learners will benefit when you use them, but especially adults with LD.

1. Break tasks down into a logical sequence of discrete steps.

2. Pre-test, teach, test, reteach, as needed, and review.

3. Provide multiple opportunities to respond, interact with the teacher and classmates, and participate. The more active the learner, the more learning is taking place.

4. Be sure mastery has been achieved before moving on to the next step in the sequence of learning tasks.

5. Provide frequent feedback that describes what was done well and how it might be improved.

6. Encourage students to tell you how they learn best, and use this information to design future lessons.

7. Use color, highlighter, enlargement of print, and underlining to strengthen the visual input and enhance visual memory.

8. De-emphasize oral reading as this may interfere with comprehension and also embarrass the student. Use oral reading only for select purposes and in private. When instruction takes place in small groups, call on students with LD only if they volunteer to participate. Preparing passages for oral reading in advance of the group instruction may help to prevent failure and embarrassment. Choral reading may be helpful.

9. De-emphasize closely timed tests and tasks.

10. Slow down the rate of your speech (assuming it is usually rapid) emphasizing important points. Maintain eye contact in order to assess level of comprehension, encourage participation, give and get feedback, and maintain attention.

11. Maximize success and enhance self-esteem by providing opportunities for the student to be successful.

12. Encourage the use of compensatory strategies (e.g., tape recording sessions, directions, assignments, and discussions) as aids for those with memory deficits.

13. Teach word processing skills, use of spelling and grammar checkers, and other software.

14. Use multi-media approaches such as audio cassette with text or video tape to preview story line of novel to supplement information from print.

15. Teach memory enhancement strategies that will aid recall such as listing, re-writing, categorizing, alphabetizing, visualizing, and use of associations and acronyms.

NEXT STEPS

The specific strategies of choice should be individualized based on the individual's profile and the effectiveness of each strategy. Instructional strategies specific to the individual's learning disability or difference are beyond the scope of LVA tutor training. However, your coordinator can schedule or inform you when there will be an in-service workshop on learning disabilities. Surely, this segment of the adult education population is one of the most challenging to work with. Therefore you may also want to reach out for assistance from your consultant and refer the adult with a suspected learning disability to specialists for a full assessment, career counseling, and further literacy training.

CHECKLIST FOR THE EVALUATION OF ADULT BASIC READING MATERIAL

WHEN FUNDS ARE LIMITED, buying wisely for the affiliate library is a must: Whenever possible, books should be reviewed with certain criteria in mind. To aid you in selecting the most useful publications, we are reprinting (with minor adaptations) the checklist developed by the Basic Education and Reading Committee of the International Reading Association (Anabel Newman and George Eyster, primary researchers; Sam Duazat, chair, 1977; Joye Jenkins Coy, chair, 1978-79).

INSTRUCTIONS

Review the adult reading material carefully. Consider, all the following in your review: the cost, the dust cover (not applicable in literacy materials), preface, table of contents, introductory instructions to the teacher and/or to the students, print, graphics, index, and all related or supporting materials.

YES NO **APPEAL**

Is the material:

❑ ❑ a. Fresh?
❑ ❑ b. Enjoyable to read?
❑ ❑ c. Of interest to adults?

RELEVANCE

Does the material:

❑ ❑ a. Pertain to adult life experience?
❑ ❑ b. Add to the general knowledge of adults?
❑ ❑ c. Present, where factual, up to date information?
❑ ❑ d. Present language naturally?

PURPOSE

Does the content:

❑ ❑ a. Include statements of broad goals and specific objectives?
❑ ❑ b. Fit the purpose of the learner?
❑ ❑ c. Fulfill a functional purpose?

PROCESS

Does the process deal with:

❑ ❑ a. Pre-reading experiences?
❑ ❑ b. Word analysis?
❑ ❑ c. Well constructed reading passages?
❑ ❑ d. A clear progression of ideas or story line?
❑ ❑ e. Comprehension?
❑ ❑ f. Appropriate vocabulary?
❑ ❑ g. Silent reading?
❑ ❑ h. Oral reading?

CHECKLIST FOR THE EVALUATION OF ADULT BASIC READING MATERIAL—*continued*

YES NO **HUMAN RELATIONS**

Does the material:

❏ ❏ a. Depict a cultural, ethnic, racial and sex group in a positive way, avoiding stereotypes?

❏ ❏ b. Represent various current occupations?

❏ ❏ c. Avoid sexist language (e.g., all male or all female nouns and pronouns) when content refers to both sexes?

❏ ❏ d. Present workers in non-stereotypical roles?

❏ ❏ e. Include characters without sexist bias?

❏ ❏ f. Stimulate interpersonal exchanges and evoke discussions?

EVALUATION

Does the material:

❏ ❏ a. Offer suggestions for continuing evaluation of the student's progress?

❏ ❏ b. Provide for pre-tests and post-tests?

FUNCTIONS OF THE MATERIAL

Does the material:

❏ ❏ a. Encourage wide reading?

❏ ❏ b. Suggest other resources and activities for student exploration?

❏ ❏ c. Promote inductive thinking?

❏ ❏ d. Provide student instructions that are clear and understandable?

❏ ❏ e. Give a sense of continuous success and mastery?

❏ ❏ f. Provide an answer key for the teacher?

❏ ❏ g. Provide an answer for the student?

YES NO **FORMAT**

Is the material format:

❏ ❏ a. Usable?

❏ ❏ b. Pleasing and attractive?

❏ ❏ c. Appealing to adult students?

❏ ❏ d. Pictorial or illustrated where appropriate (photographs, drawings, graphs, maps, etc.)?

❏ ❏ e. Presented with ample space between lines and in margins for easy reading?

❏ ❏ f. Set in type (large or medium) appropriate for the material and the student?

TEACHER DIRECTIONS

Are instructions:

❏ ❏ a. Included for the instructor where needed?

❏ ❏ b. Presented in a self-contained manual where needed?

❏ ❏ c. For the instructor clear where needed?

❏ ❏ d. Included and designed so that teachers do not need special training?

CONTENT

Judgments based upon stated or apparent readability level or design (e.g., 0-3, 3-8, 8-12 grades).

❏ ❏ a. Do the materials provide for appropriate reading level experiences?

❏ ❏ b. Are the selections short enough to hold interest and long enough to give meaning?

❏ ❏ c. Is there recognition of the amount of reinforcement needed at the content reading level?

❏ ❏ d. Does the readability develop at an appropriate rate and by increments?

❏ ❏ e. Are there comprehension exercises included?

❏ ❏ f. Are problem-solving selections included?

❏ ❏ g. Are writing activities included and linked to reading selections?

LESSON PLAN

Student Name _____ Lesson # _____

Tutor Name _____ Length of Lesson _____

Date of Lesson _____

Lesson Goal/Objectives _____

_____

Review Homework _____

_____

Work in Progress	*This Session*	*Next Session*
Language Experience _____	_____	_____
Writing _____	_____	_____
Reading _____	_____	_____
Workbook _____	_____	_____
Other _____	_____	_____
_____	_____	_____

Trigger Materials as Needed

_____ _____ _____

Comprehension

_____ _____ _____

_____ _____ _____

Questions/Discussion (Before, During, After)

_____ _____ _____

_____ _____ _____

Writing Comments

_____ _____ _____

_____ _____ _____

_____ _____ _____

LESSON PLAN—*continued*

Direct Instruction (from Reading/Writing)	*This Session*	*Next Session*
Sight Words		
Phonics		
Word Patterns		
Multi-Syllabic Words		
Spelling		

Reinforcement for Direct Instruction		
Workbooks—Subskills		
Games, Puzzles, etc.		

Student Evaluation		

Homework Assignment		

Model Reading		
Selection—Title, Pages		

Student Comments

Tutor Notes (assessment, observation)

LESSON PLAN

Student Name _____   Lesson # _____

Tutor Name _____   Length of Lesson _____

Date of Lesson _____

Lesson Goal/Objectives _____

_____

Review Homework _____

_____

	This Session	*Next Session*
_____	_____	_____
_____	_____	_____
_____	_____	_____
_____	_____	_____
_____	_____	_____
_____	_____	_____
_____	_____	_____
_____	_____	_____
_____	_____	_____
_____	_____	_____
_____	_____	_____
_____	_____	_____
_____	_____	_____

Student Comments

_____   _____   _____

_____   _____   _____

Tutor Notes (assessment, observation)

_____   _____   _____

_____   _____   _____

_____   _____   _____

BIBLIOGRAPHY

Abercrombie, M.L.J. (1964). *Anatomy of judgment: An investigation into the processes of perception and reading.* New York: Basic Books.

Applebee, A.N. (1981). *Writing in the secondary school: English and the content areas.* Urbana: National Council of Teachers of English (NCTE).

Applebee, A., & Langer, J. (1983). Instructional scaffolding: Reading and writing as natural language activities. *Language Arts,* 60, 168-75.

Bruffee, K. (1973). Collaborative learning: Some practical models. *College English, 34,* 579-586.

Bruffee, K. (1986). Social construction, language, and the authority of knowledge: A bibliographical essay. *College English, 48(8),* 773-788.

Bruner, J. (1986). *Actual minds, possible worlds.* Cambridge: Harvard University Press.

Clifford, J. (1981). Composing in stages: The effects of a collaborative pedagogy. *Research in the Teaching of English, 1,* 37-53.

Connolly, P., and Vilardi, T. (Ed.). (1989). *Writing to learn mathematics and science.* New York: Teachers College Press, Columbia University.

Cooper, C. (1977). Holistic evaluation of writing. In C. Cooper and L. Odell (Eds.), *Evaluating writing: describing, measuring, judging.* Urbana: NCTE.

Diederich, P. (1974). *Measuring growth in English.* Urbana: NCTE.

Emig, J. (1971). *The composing processes of twelfth graders.* Urbana: NCTE.

Enos, T. (Ed.). (1987). *A source book for basic writing teachers.* New York: Random House.

Farrell, T. (1977). Literacy, the basics, and all that jazz. *College Composition and Communication, 38,* 443-449.

Flower, L., & Hayes, J. (1981). A cognitive process theory of writing. *College Composition and Communication, 32,* 365-387.

Foster, D. (1983). *A primer for writing teachers.* Upper Montclair, N.J.: Boynton/Cook.

Fromkin, V., and Rodman, R. (1993). *An introduction to language.* 5th Edition. New York: Harcourt Brace Jovanovich.

George, D. (1984). Working with peer groups in the composition classroom. *College Composition and Communication, 35,* 320-326.

Greenbaum, S. (1989). *A college grammar of English.* New York: Longman.

Hartwell, P. (1985). Grammar, grammars, and the teaching of grammar. *College English, 47,* 105-127.

Hillocks, G. (1982). The interaction of instruction, teacher comment, and revision in teaching the composition process. *Research in the Teaching of English, 16(3),* 261-78.

Hillocks, G. (1986). *Research on written composition: New directions for teaching.* Urbana: ERIC Clearinghouse on Reading and Communication Skills and National Conference on Research in English.

Hoyt, F. (1906). The place of grammar in the elementary curriculum. *Teachers College Record, 7,* 483-84.

Kirsch, I., and Jungeblut, A. (1987). *Literacy: Profiles of America's young adults.* Princeton, N.J: NAEP, Educational Testing Service.

Kucera, H., and Francis, W.N. (1967). *Computational analysis of present-day American English.* Providence, RI: Brown University Press.

Lunsford, A. (1978). What we know—and don't know—about remedial writing. *College Composition and Communication, 29,* 47-52.

BIBLIOGRAPHY—*continued*

Lunsford, A. (1979). Cognitive development and the basic writer. *College English, 41*, 38-46.

Macrorie, K. (1984). *Writing to be read* (3rd Edition). Rochelle, N.J.: Hayden.

Miller, S. (1983). *Special reading problems*. Syracuse, NY: Literacy Volunteers of America, Inc.

Moffett, J. (1976). *Student-centered language arts and reading*. Boston: Houghton Mifflin.

Murray, D. (1978). Write before writing. *College Composition and Communication, 29*, 375-81.

Myers, M. (1980). *A procedure for writing assessment and holistic scoring*. Urbana: ERIC Clearinghouse on Reading and Communication Skills and the NCTE.

Myers, M. (1985). *The teacher-researcher: How to study writing in the classroom*. Urbana: ERIC Clearinghouse on Reading and Communication Skills and the NCTE.

Northcutt, N. (1975). *The adult performance level study*. Austin, TX: University of Texas.

Perl, S. (1979). The composing processes of unskilled college writers. *Research in the Teaching of English, 13*, 317-336.

Piaget, J. (1954). *The construction of reality in the child*. New York: Basic Books.

Rose, M. (1980). Rigid rules, inflexible plans, and the stifling of language: A cognitivist analysis of writer's block. *College Composition and Communication, 31*, 389-99.

Rose, M. (1984). *Writer's block: The cognitive dimension*. Carbondale: Southern Illinois University Press.

Rosenblatt, L. (1978). *The reader, the text, the poem*. Carbondale: Southern Illinois University Press.

Shaughnessy, M. (1976a). Basic Writing. In G. Fate (Ed.) *Teaching composition: 10 biographical essays*. Fort Worth: Texas Christian University Press.

Shaughnessy, M. (1976b). Diving in: An introduction to basic writing. *College Composition and Communication, 27*, 234-30.

Shaughnessy, M. (1977). *Errors and expectations: A guide for the teacher of basic writing*. New York: Oxford University Press.

Sommers, N. (1980). Revision strategies of student writers and experienced writers. *College Composition and Communication, 31*, 378-88.

Vygotsky, L. (1962). *Thought and language* (E. Hanfmann & G. Vakar, Trans.). Cambridge: M.I.T.

Wangberg, E., et al. (1984). First steps toward an adult word list. *Journal of Reading*. International Reading Association.

Weaver, C. (1988). *Reading process and practice*. Portsmouth, NH: Heinemann.

Weiner, H. (1986). Collaborative learning in the classroom: A guide to evaluation. *College English, 48*, 52-61.

Wertsch, J., et al. (1980). The adult-child dyad as a problem solving system. *Child development, 51*, 1215-21.

West, F. (1975). *The way of language*. New York: Harcourt Brace Jovanovich.

Wilde, S. (1989). Understanding spelling strategies. In K. Goodman and Y. Goodman (Eds.). *The whole language evaluation book*. Portsmouth, NH: Heinemann.

Wilde, S. (1992). *You kan red this!* Portsmouth, NH: Heinemann.

TO ORDER MATERIALS

New Readers Press
ProLiteracy™ Worldwide

Department SP3
P.O. Box 35888
Syracuse, New York 13235-5888
(800) 448-8878
(866) 894-2100 (fax)
www.newreaderspress.com